Cambridge Elements ☰

Elements in Critical H
edited l
Kristian Kristiansen, *Unive.*
Michael Rowlands, *UCL*
Francis Nyamnjoh, *University of Cape Town*
Astrid Swenson, *Bath University*
Shu-Li Wang, *Academia Sinica*
Ola Wetterberg, *University of Gothenburg*

HERITAGE, EDUCATION AND SOCIAL JUSTICE

Veysel Apaydin
University College London

CAMBRIDGE
UNIVERSITY PRESS

Shaftesbury Road, Cambridge CB2 8EA, United Kingdom

One Liberty Plaza, 20th Floor, New York, NY 10006, USA

477 Williamstown Road, Port Melbourne, VIC 3207, Australia

314–321, 3rd Floor, Plot 3, Splendor Forum, Jasola District Centre, New Delhi – 110025, India

103 Penang Road, #05–06/07, Visioncrest Commercial, Singapore 238467

Cambridge University Press is part of Cambridge University Press & Assessment, a department of the University of Cambridge.

We share the University's mission to contribute to society through the pursuit of education, learning and research at the highest international levels of excellence.

www.cambridge.org
Information on this title: www.cambridge.org/9781009055543

DOI: 10.1017/9781009052351

First published 2022

A catalogue record for this publication is available from the British Library.

ISBN 978-1-009-05554-3 Paperback
ISSN 2632-7074 (online)
ISSN 2632-7066 (print)

Heritage, Education and Social Justice

Elements in Critical Heritage Studies

DOI: 10.1017/9781009052351
First published online: November 2022

Veysel Apaydin
University College London
Author for correspondence: Veysel Apaydin, v.apaydin@ucl.ac.uk

Abstract: This research examines how museums and heritage sites can embrace a social justice approach to tackle inequalities and how they can empower disadvantaged groups to take an equal benefit from cultural resources. This Element argues that heritage institutions can use their collections of material culture more effectively to respond to social issues, and examines how they can promote equal access to resources for all people, regardless of their backgrounds. This research examines heritage and museum practices, ranging from critical and democratic approaches to authoritarian practices to expose the pitfalls and potentials therein. By analysing case studies, examining institutions' current efforts and suggesting opportunities for further development with regard to social justice, this Element argues that heritage sites and museums have great potential to tackle social issues and to create a platform for the equal redistribution of cultural resources, the recognition of diversities and the representation of diverse voices.

Keywords: heritage, museum, education, social justice, inequalities

ISBNs: 9781009055543 (PB), 9781009052351 (OC)
ISSNs: 2632-7074 (online), 2632-7066 (print)

Contents

1 Introduction

Over the last decade, through my research and fieldwork, I have engaged with many heritage sites and museums and their education programmes across Europe. In Turkey and the United Kingdom, I conducted ethnographic fieldwork to evaluate the role of heritage and museums as social and cultural spaces, and have examined education programmes to analyse levels of engagement and their impact on diverse communities and audiences. While some museums and heritage sites in the United Kingdom and other parts of Europe have a more democratic approach to education through participatory models in their displays and programmes, Turkey's approach to heritage and museum displays is far more top down, whereby communities are excluded from decision-making processes and from participating in the design of such programmes. This difference can also be seen when looking at the representation of diverse communities. UK museum and heritage practices in particular have shifted to a more representative model with the inclusion of multiple narratives and diverse histories. This can especially be seen in small and community museum practices. In contrast, such movement towards more multivalent and representative practices is rarely found in Turkey.

In this Element I address the heritage and museum practices of both countries. In my research projects, especially in Turkey, I have come across extreme uses of top-down approaches by museums and heritage sites. This is an impact of Turkey's political system, which has become increasingly authoritarian in the last two decades (Brown 2019). In 2010, I went to Ani, a medieval Armenian site that still contains substantial architecture and monuments and is located in the East of Turkey, close to the Armenian border. Here I aimed to examine how minority ethnic groups' heritage is treated in Turkey.

Ani has been excavated by Turkish archaeologists for decades and most of its artefacts are displayed at the Kars Museum, which is in the nearest town. The first time I went to visit the museum to collect data and interview museum professionals, one thing was extremely clear: the word 'Armenian' was carefully avoided in the museum displays. This undermining (and arguably manipulative) approach against other minority communities in Turkey can be seen in many other state museums. This is a reflection of Turkish nationalism, which began in the early years of the Republic but has become increasingly obvious in the last two decades. In particular, ethnic Turkish heritage has been given more attention than these other groups in order to consolidate an official Turkish ideology of national identity (Zencirci 2014).

Another example of how my experiences shaped this Element is that for many years, my MA students and I have run workshops with London's museums and heritage sites – for example, at Hackney Museum – that reflect upon diversity, recognition and representation of social justice through these sites' displays and education programmes. In this we use the museum as a space to reflect on social, historical and political issues and reflect on best practices. In these visits as well as through years of observations, ethnographic fieldwork, discussions and conversations with my students and museum professionals it had become clear to me that we need more effective social justice–based approaches and practices to better support communities, and as heritage and museum researchers and professionals, that we need to take a more determined role in social, cultural and political life. Throughout this Element, I return to the following core themes: how heritage sites and museums can support communities' well-being and sustainability; how these sites can act as agents to provide support for developing skills; how heritage sites and museums can better reflect on social, political, economic and historical issues to develop dialogues between communities; how they can act to reduce inequalities that have developed over centuries that still need to be discussed and researched and how such sites can develop creative methods to enable these issues to be addressed and resolved.

Over the last two decades, heritage and museum practices have significantly progressed through the development of a range of methods to more directly engage the public in curatorial and educational activities (Macdonald 2006; Janes and Sandell 2019). To move beyond the colonial and ideological roles of heritage and museums, in place of the top-down decision-making processes traditionally used, appeals have also been made to make heritage and museums more public and participatory in their practices. Additionally, in some parts of the world, social and political issues have begun to be tackled more directly in the field of heritage and museum studies.

For instance, in Australia and Canada, dealing with historical, political and social issues in the context of indigenous heritage and rights can clearly be seen. This also is reflected in these countries' heritage, museum and learning practices, as some indigenous communities are managing their own heritage (Nicholas and Smith 2020). This stands in contrast to traditional, authoritarian and oppressive heritage practices in undemocratic nation states that exclude diversity and increase inequalities and social injustices. However, in those countries, where the social justice approach is lacking, we see increasing grassroots heritage movements. The recent grassroots movement in Turkey, which mounted resistance to the demolition of Gezi Park in the centre of Istanbul (see Apaydin 2020b for more discussions about Gezi Park), is a good example. This clearly demonstrated that top-down or authoritarian approaches to heritage create tension between the people and the state. This results from dissonance in how meanings and values of heritage differ at a local or popular level as compared to the vision of the state (see Apaydin 2018 for Turkey; Evans and Rowlands 2021 for China). This type of top-down approach also fuels inequalities and injustices by excluding communities from their own heritage and by consuming, using and abusing their cultural resources, as in the case of Turkey.

In response to such challenges this research focuses on how heritage sites and museums can tackle the issues around inequalities and injustices, particularly in the design, development and delivery of education programmes and museum displays, and in the use of heritage sites and museums as social–political and cultural spaces to respond to injustices. *Heritage, Education and Social Justice* considers heritage sites and museums as not only places where the public can have fun and learn about the history and the past, but also as crucial concepts and social, economic and cultural spaces that have the power to reflect on the injustices and inequalities of wider society. To do this, the Element explores the concept and practice of social justice and how it plays a crucial role in a heritage and museum context.

Social justice has been defined differently in many political spheres and the social sciences, all of which have framed it in relation to their respective fields and agendas. For example, in the heritage and museum context, Charlotte Joy, in her recent book, *Heritage Justice* (2020), clearly demonstrates how justice can reflect in repatriation and restitution contexts in relation to objects and artefacts in European museums that were brought from the Global South. This is an understanding of social justice and a contextualisation of it in museums from a legal perspective and ethical approaches related mainly to restitution. While important, I discuss social justice in this research differently and define it as equal access to and distribution of wealth and resources; equal and fair opportunities in social, economic, cultural and political life, regardless of economic, social, political, cultural and identity backgrounds; and as having an equal voice in decision-making processes (see Fraser 2003) in the heritage and museum context (see Fraser 2003). Thus, building on this core definition, my main focus is on the value and rights of local and disadvantaged groups and to consider the role of education and museums to support and empower these groups to develop skills and take equal part in social, cultural and political life.

In this Element I lay out the values of 'anti-oppressive' (Bell 2016) heritage and museum practice that recognise diversities, advocate equality and that aim to prevent all forms of prejudice, racism and bias. In this way, I argue that the main social role of museums and heritage practice is to provide the groundwork for developing sustainable and equal societies. To support this, this Element critically examines Pierre Bourdieu's concepts of 'the forms of capital' and 'habitus' (1984, 1986, 2005), Iris Marion Young's forms of 'oppression' (1990), Paulo Freire's concept of 'dialogue' (1970) and Nancy Fraser's social justice concepts, particularly 'recognition', 'redistribution' and 'representation' (1997, 2000, 2003, 2009, 2013), and situating them in the heritage and museum context.

I focus on the theories of these thinkers as a means to draw out their critical reflections on inequalities and injustices throughout the twentieth and twenty-first centuries and show how these might help to elucidate discourses of injustices that heavily affected understanding and use of heritage and museums. *Heritage, Education and Social Justice* takes a strong interdisciplinary approach and draws on intensive theoretical and practical research. To do this I examine a range of case studies across Europe. The focal point of comparison is between the United Kingdom – which prides itself on being at the forefront of heritage practice – and Turkey, which has become an extremely authoritarian nation state in the last two decades with consequent effects on heritage and museum practices.

I examine current practices in light of my own recent ethnographic fieldwork on heritage sites and museums in the United Kingdom and Turkey. This includes investigation of people-centred museum practices that utilise digital tools for onsite and offsite experiences. While the use of digital tools can be encouraging for learning and engaging audiences both at and away from museum and sites, they are also a crucial part of redistribution of knowledge to wider audiences as part of social justice. That said, digital media and online engagement can create new forms of exclusion that need to be considered (Robinson et al. 2015) because a large proportion of society does not have access to the skills to use digital tools (i.e., digital poverty; I return to this in Section 2).

By focusing on key aspects of social justice – particularly the roles of recognition, representation, redistribution that were developed and discussed by Nancy Fraser (2003, 2009) – I will outline a critical toolkit to understand social justice in the heritage and museum contexts, and offer a way forward to design and develop social justice–focused heritage and museum practices and education programmes alongside effective, critical and constructive people-centred engagement strategies. Although I will delve into social justice and its dimensions more deeply in Section 4, for context here, the dimension of **recognition** seeks to acknowledge all differences in the society from ethnic backgrounds to gender differences; the **representation** dimension looks at how diverse voices can be brought into the decision-making process as part of democratic approach and **redistribution** seeks equal distribution of wealth and resources.

My main aims in this Element are to contextualise these social justice dimensions in the heritage context by critically reflecting on how heritage sites and museums can be spaces where all differences are recognised; how heritage sites and museums as spaces transfer their power to the people who then manage these cultural settings, from curatorial practices to education programmes (as I consider this a starting point of achieving social justice in heritage and museum contexts) and how all communities, regardless of their ethnic, gender, economic and/or educational backgrounds, are able to obtain an equal and equitable share from the knowledge that is produced, stored and used in heritage sites and museums. While I aim to contextualise social justice in heritage sites and museum settings, I also specifically aim to analyse questions that are more related to current education and learning programmes at heritage sites and museums: How can these education programmes be shifted in terms of their designs and content to meet community needs and priorities? Can they provide the groundwork for communities to develop skills to actively take a greater role in social, political and economic life so inequalities are reduced rather than developing these education programmes in parallel to expert and institutional agendas? I also refer to a question about criticality in education: Who is education for? Is it for the protection and preservation of material culture of the past only? Or is it for people who need to have an equal access to cultural settings and, therefore, access to education to develop skills and thus take equal distribution from cultural capital? And importantly, how does the content of these education programmes help to develop critical consciousness to prevent all forms of racism, prejudice and discrimination in today's world?

In the heritage and museum context, social justice can be manifested and constructed in different ways, from the design and development of exhibitions to education programmes and community and public engagement, and the sharing of the power of heritage and museums as institutions. Most importantly, social justice is about using heritage sites and museums as a space where people's voices can be heard, not only about heritage and museum work and issues but also about wider social, political and economic issues that create inequalities in society. In other words, using heritage and museums in parallel to reflect on needs, priorities and agendas of communities rather than those of institutions and experts. Throughout this Element, I will argue that heritage sites and museums, as a space, can use their collections and material culture to respond to contemporary social and political issues and to draw on social justice concepts and promote equal access to resources, justice and well-being for all people, regardless of their social, ethnic, gender, sexual, political and economic backgrounds, in order to develop dialogues between communities to discuss contemporary and historical issues.

The material culture in the care or otherwise connected with heritage and museum institutions can act as a powerful resource for individuals and communities. Adapted from the perspectives of memory, identity, well-being and belonging, these are particularly vital aspects for communities and minority ethnic groups at risk of discrimination or even disappearing (see Butler 2006; Smith 2006, 2021; Harrison 2013; Apaydin 2018, 2020a). This is even true for archaeological heritage, which has the potential to show us alternative ways of social, cultural, political and economic life and possibilities of creating sustainable and peaceful futures drawn from new insights about the past (see Graeber and Wengrow 2021).

In this Element, I will discuss a framework for the concept of social justice adapted specifically to the museum and heritage context. Although scholars (e.g., Coffee 2008; Sandell and Nightingale 2012; Kinsley 2016; Lynch 2021) reflect on social justice and the social role of museums, the question of what social justice is, in a wider social and political context and how it is situated from heritage, museum and material culture perspectives, needs more exploration and discussion (see Joy 2020). The oppressive forces that create inequalities and injustices and the 'redistribution', 'recognition' and 'representation' dimensions of social justice in particular need further analysis and exploration. By recognising important aspects of both group and individual identities through the creation of spaces and opportunities for education, museums and sites become crucial community spaces where new meanings and memories can be ascribed and developed as sites of activism, especially for disadvantaged, economically deprived and socially and politically discriminated groups.

The increased social inequalities, pervasive in every aspect of life, have also influenced museum and heritage institutions which had once been spaces only for certain groups that held higher levels of social, cultural and economic capital. While current practices in some museums offer innovative learning opportunities through presenting visual and intangible practices and material culture, as well as through creating virtual cultural experiences using digital tools, the understanding and application of the role of social justice in heritage and museums are still broadly lacking. This lack of understanding of social justice and its applications can be seen in many large museums across the globe, where the past and contemporary material culture is displayed as primarily separate from the concerns of contemporary societies. However, the 'old museology' and these more traditional museum practices, which retain heavy traces of colonial and nationalist approaches (see Bennett 1995, 2017; Bennett et al. 2017), are nonetheless shifting in terms of curatorial and managerial practices (see Janes and Sandell 2019; Lynch 2021), especially through some grassroots movements (i.e., in terms of community and social issues engagement) and small community museum practices. Examples of this include the 'museums are not neutral'[1] movement that advocates the potential of museums to engage with social and political issues that communities face and act as agents for positive change in society. Other important examples are found in the 'decolonising museums' debates that many Western museums, of former western imperial powers, have faced recently and museum and heritage practices that consider issues of migration and homelessness, such as the Museum of Homelessness[2] and Hackney Museum in the United Kingdom.[3] Additionally, the increasing nationalism across Europe and Turkey is pushing heritage and museum practice – from displays to education programmes to public engagement – to take more responsibility and reflect on contested histories and to present social, political and economic issues.

Although there are good examples that directly engage with social inequalities and injustices, it is crucial to expose how heritage sites and museums can take more responsibility and play a part in challenging and preventing prejudices and racism and, in doing so, also make material culture and heritage and museum spaces more accessible to wider and more diverse audiences. This is especially necessary for those who have been deprived from social, economic and cultural life. Therefore, it is crucial to analyse whether current heritage and museum practices are critical in reflecting on social and political issues; how heritage and museums can provide support for disadvantaged, deprived and discriminated groups; how heritage sites and museums as an educational tool can be used to respond to the changing social, political and economic parameters in the world; to understand what methods can be developed to make heritage and museums act as social and cultural agents that empower individuals, groups and communities, regardless of their backgrounds, to develop organisational skills and knowledge to create equal, sustainable societies.

In today's world, with increasingly intense use of neoliberal policies across the world, archaeology, heritage and museums have an important role because social and economic inequality is increasing and impacting every individual and group, especially disadvantaged people and groups who are deprived of their basic human rights (e.g., access to food, water, health, education, shelter). These are the 'people's priorities' that need to be dealt with, according to the recent survey by United Nations. In particular, exclusion from equal access to education leads to inequalities for communities that span generations prevents people from developing the skills to take part in economic and cultural life (Bourdieu 2005) and leads to oppression and poverty, as Freire (1970) demonstrated in the case of the poorest and most underdeveloped areas of north east Brazil.

---

[1] See www.museumsarenotneutral.com/.   [2] See https://museumofhomelessness.org/.
[3] See https://hackney-museum.hackney.gov.uk.

Education acts as major resource for communities and heritage sites and museums are important informal education spaces, linked to cultural, social and economic resources or, in other words, they hold 'capital' as Bourdieu (1986) explains. This is also linked to Bourdieu's concept of 'habitus'. According to Bourdieu, habitus can be anywhere where people interact with each other, it can be used in daily life or for economic and political purposes and where knowledge is produced (Bourdieu 2005, 43):

> ... habitus is a system of disposition, that is of permanent manners of being, seeing, acting and thinking or a system of long lasting (rather than permanent) schemes of schemata or structures of perception, conception and action ...

In other words, what Bourdieu emphasises is that habitus is social, cultural, economic and political as in the case of heritage sites, museums and galleries. I stress this link because heritage sites and museums are being used as social and cultural spaces for social and cultural production. In order to elucidate the concept and use of habitus, Bourdieu (1986) discusses three types of capital: 'economic', 'social' and 'cultural'. It is the relative lack and unequal access to these forms of capital that are the main causes of inequality and injustices in today's world.

Bourdieu's concept of economic capital is based on materiality, which can be anything that has economic value and can be converted into money or profit making. This is a capitalist definition of materiality and is highly linked to mass consumption (Miller 2005). This is widely explored in the heritage and museum context (see Mazzanti 2003; Mason 2008) and on a basic level, is related to the question of the economic value of heritage sites: how do they make a profit, especially through tourism? This is because material culture and heritage sites are part of a broader consumerist culture, particularly with the intense use of neoliberal policies over the last few decades (see Harvey 2005), which has increased the unequal sharing of wealth and resources among individuals and communities. In a heritage and museum context, this is linked to the questions of economic value for whom, and around who benefits from economic capital? These questions have largely been neglected as local communities have frequently been excluded from the economic benefits of heritage sites (see also Zhu 2021). For instance, in Turkey where museums and heritage sites are controlled centrally (Baraldi et al. 2013), all such sites' income goes to the central government. Even if tourism and income increase, local communities are only seeing limited benefits (Apaydin 2016b).

This also highlights the links and importance of social capital which Bourdieu (1986) defines as 'possession of a durable network of more or less institutionalised relationship of mutual acquaintance and recognition – or in other words, to membership in a group'. In other words, social capital provides resources for individuals and groups to gain power and status and therefore have a voice in social and economic life. Heritage sites, museums and other forms of cultural settings are spaces where individual and collective identities and memories are developed or, in other words, these spaces play an important role in 'social production' (Lefebvre 1991). Considering heritage sites, museums and galleries where knowledge of material culture is stored and displayed, we need to give more attention to who accesses this social capital and to make it more accessible to all, regardless of background. This is import- ant because heritage sites, museums and galleries are mostly accessed by certain classes who also hold higher levels of economic capital. For instance, the *Taking Part* surveys[4] demonstrate that more deprived populations within the United Kingdom access and use heritage sites, museums and galleries far less than economically more prosperous areas. Likewise, the *City Household Survey* in 2011 (Ipsos MORI 2011) also showed inequality in those using museums: community members from the most deprived areas of Glasgow used museums and galleries far less than community members from the wealthy areas of the city. Research conducted by Nick Merriman (1991), more than three decades ago, also showed that museum visitors come from well-educated or high-status groups (also see O'Neill 2021).

Although in Turkey there is no detailed data about who visits these cultural settings, the Turkish Statistical Institute shows access to museums city by city and it can be seen that the western cities of Turkey that are more developed economically provide access to museums and sites much more than poorer areas (see Tuik 2020). Therefore, we as heritage researchers and practitioners, need to focus more on how we can make these cultural settings more accessible to diverse audiences.

While unequal use and access of and to museums and heritage sites is linked to social and economic capital, it is also strongly interrelated with cultural capital. Bourdieu (1986, 18–19) defines two types of cultural capital: 'the embodied cultural capital', which is linked to the unequal access to opportun- ities of institutional resources (e.g., education); and 'the objectified state', which refers to 'material objects and media such as writings, painting, monu- ments, instruments, etc., ... transmissible in its materiality'. In the heritage context, I confer this second type to cultural goods, production and material culture that are vital for communities. The second type also has social, eco- nomic and cultural value for individuals and groups who develop skills and knowledge through the material culture of the past and present, which are placed in heritage sites or displayed at museums and other cultural settings.

---

[4] See the Taking Part Surveys: www.artscouncil.org.uk/taking-part-survey.

In this sense, I would argue that two types of skills linked to cultural capital can be identified in the heritage and museum context: (1) skills that people already have to be able to understand and engage with the material culture, heritage and museums and get the most from museum and heritage visit; and (2) skills the individual gains from visiting cultural settings and institutions, such as improving their knowledge of their society, their ability to contribute to debates, political consciousness, critical thinking and comprehension – transferable skills that help individuals to be stronger economically and culturally in society. While Bourdieu's reflections on cultural capital lead some groups to use material culture for their development and sustainability, it also draws a line between those groups and the disadvantaged groups, who are economically, socially and culturally deprived from these resources.

As discussed in Bourdieu's theory of capital, groups that hold economic power are also able to form, reshape and control social and cultural life. This idea of the influence of capital is strongly bound up with the concept of 'oppression', which creates inequal access to heritage and museum settings as well as introduces inequality in using material culture as an educational and cultural resource which is an established right. Political theorist Iris Marion Young (1990, 41) discusses 'oppression' when describing injustices and points out that "oppressions are systematically reproduced in major economic, political, and cultural institutions". She emphasises 'five faces of oppression: exploitation, marginalization, powerlessness, cultural imperialism and violence', and shows how oppression itself is also an inequality as people are exploited through their labour and marginalised with their world views, backgrounds and identities and, therefore, become powerless as they are deprived of using resources. She also discusses how cultural resources are consumed or colonised and how people have been under threat because of their race or religious beliefs (see Young 1990 for more about oppression). In this Element, I take the example of Turkey to illustrate this, where this kind of oppression can be more clearly seen because of the intensive use of neoliberalism, nationalism and authoritarianism (see Brown 2019). In this context, groups that hold economic power oppress the 'other' or minority ethnic groups by not recognising their economic, social and cultural rights – including race, ethnicity, sexuality and gender – in heritage and museum settings or any cultural spaces, and this is linked to the redistribution and recognition dimensions of social justice. Therefore, as Fraser (2003) emphasises, both the redistribution and recognition concepts need to be considered together for social justice to overcome the main features of oppression.

The 'five faces of oppression' as defined by Young are strongly reflected in museum and heritage institutions and, whether intentionally or not, as heritage and museum professionals and academics, we have supported this kind of oppression over the decades. This attitude can especially be seen in neglecting and misrecognising minority and disadvantaged groups' heritage as in the case of Turkey's all-state museums (Girard 2015) and some of the USA's museums (Coffee 2008; Kinsley 2016), for example. This type of systematic and structural oppressive approach became common in every aspect of life but can be seen most clearly in the context of education (Bell 2016), which may be the most powerful tool to fuel division, inequalities and injustices as well as to increase racism and discrimination. Considering heritage and museum settings, as a whole, as educational spaces where the public can learn, develop knowledge and transform this learning and knowledge into cultural, social and economic skills, it is important to delve into discourses of education.

Formal education is perhaps one of the most influential and effective tools to form and reshape the public because it is generally compulsory across the world and it's also usually shaped in parallel to state ideologies or interests of the groups who hold power. Educator and philosopher Paulo Freire, who was an advocate of critical pedagogy, elucidates the roles and methods of oppressor and the oppressed, and their reflection in the education system. He points out (Freire 1970, 60):

> ... the oppressors are using science and technology as unquestionably powerful instruments for their purpose: the maintenance of the oppressive order through manipulation and repression. The oppressed, as objects, as 'things', have no purposes except those their oppressors prescribe for them.

The main features of the social justice education approach and design lie in exposing and challenging the inequalities and injustices. The first principles of social justice education were established in the early twentieth century with the reflection on the concept of democracy and its interrelation with formal education. John Dewey (1954) approached issues of inequalities and injustices by emphasising the importance of democratic education in schools to overcome oppression, which was further detailed in the education context by Bell (2016), where she outlines and situates 'features of oppression'. Bell (2016, 5) describes 'oppression' as "restrictive, pervasive, and cumulative; socially constructed, categorising, and group-based; hierarchical, normalised, and hegemonic; intersectional and internalised; and durable and mutable". These features of oppression, of course, fuel inequalities and injustices for disadvantaged groups. I am not going to delve into each feature here but I will contextualise these characteristics of oppression below as they all play a role in heritage and museum practices. However, what's important in working towards social justice practices is that how we design heritage and museum practices and education programmes to challenge these oppressive features or injustices and inequalities.

In current education systems, in many parts of the world, most features of oppression can be seen in many different contexts. For instance, in the Turkish formal education system, the content of textbooks is intentionally designed to neglect or misrecognise minority heritage (Apaydin 2016c). This is particularly the case for Kurds, Armenians and Greeks in Turkey because they are considered to be a threat to national unity, and texts are full of prejudice, biases and hate speech. This kind of state-sanctioned 'knowledge' included in textbooks and museums also occurs in China (Denton 2014). Even in the case of the USA, for example, educational portrayals of different groups were socially constructed with categories based on simplistic depictions of their identities (race, class, gender, sexuality) that are contextualised with historical and geographical perspectives, with a one-sided history, and presented at schools (Bell 2016). So how does this type of structural oppression, which leads to inequalities and injustices, impact heritage and museum practices?

To respond to this and previous questions, in Section 2, I will look at current heritage and museums practices from display approaches to designing and delivering education programmes and engagement strategies, using case studies. Whilst I will look at creative and critical museum and heritage practices, I will also discuss the authoritarian use of heritage and museum practices along with global and digital ones and I will demonstrate that digital practices have actually increased inequalities in terms of using and accessing cultural resources. In Section 3, my focus will shift more towards 'criticality' and I will discuss how museums and heritage sites can be used as spaces for developing dialogues that can lead to the development of critical approaches and critical literacies. How heritage sites and museums can be used as 'contact zones' (Clifford 1997) and places where communities can negotiate historical issues and reflect on present social, economic and political problems, and enable critical collaboration between heritage sites, museums and communities. Here, drawing on Paulo Freire's *Pedagogy of Oppressed*, I will attempt to demonstrate how heritage sites and museums can be taken over by people who then contribute to museum literacies by displaying and designing education programmes and by using museums and heritage sites as community spaces. I consider this to be one of the main foundations of social justice. This will be linked to Section 4 where I delve into three dimensions of social justice: 'redistribution, recognition and representations', which were developed by political philosopher Nancy Fraser (1998, 2003), in order to contextualise these concepts in heritage and museum settings and to attempt to create a framework through case studies. In Section 5, I conclude and reflect on the previous sections and make suggestions for social justice heritage practice in the future.

2 Heritage and Museum Practices: Pitfalls and Potentials

Despite museum and heritage education becoming very popular and many museums and heritage institutions engaging with this crucial area (see Hooper-Greenhill 2007; Lynch 2016; Falk and Dierking 2018), heritage and museum practices and education need to be reconceptualised and rethought in terms of the approaches and methods in engaging with their audiences in order to develop effective and successful education programmes to help to reduce inequalities that are structural in today's world. However consciously or unconsciously, heritage sites and museums have contributed to increasing inequalities for decades. In other words, heritage and museums as institutions, in many parts of the world, have become agents of inequalities themselves. Therefore, we need to ask questions about how heritage and museum researchers and practitioners act in designing displays and education programmes and how their work outcomes contribute to inequalities and oppression. Museum and heritage platforms, as informal learning spaces, however, have the potential to break down these inequalities by delivering knowledge that is ascribed to the material culture to wider communities and to create dialogues between cultures and communities (see Hein 2005).

In mainstream current heritage and museum practices, critical education programmes, from design to delivery and reaching wider and diverse audiences and in terms of decreasing inequalities in the content of these programmes, have largely been neglected, though there are some good examples emerging in the United Kingdom (e.g., Hackney Museum, Horniman Museum), which are designed to engage with injustices and critical components of heritage from a people-centred perspective rather than top-down approaches (discussed in the last part of this section). 'Criticality', as I refer to it here, is how heritage institutions and museums constructively deal with social, political and economic issues (see Winter 2013) and provide the grounding for the development of disadvantaged groups and how they can use people-centred methods more effectively in terms of power sharing.

I define the 'people-centred approach' as a model that requires strong collaboration with community members and the public in heritage and museum projects. In this model, heritage and museum specialists consider community cohesion with diverse backgrounds, community needs and priorities and include communities in every stage of the projects where communities make the decisions, rather than experts. Social, cultural and material practices are important aspects of developing communities and make the tangible and intangible heritage that are core sources of heritage sites and museums. Therefore, heritage and museum specialists need to rethink methods to effectively involve communities in heritage and museum practices. This is more about how to democratise museum and heritage practices from designing displays to exhibitions and education programmes and it is strongly bounded with the 'representation' dimension of social justice, which I will explore more in Section 4.

In contrast, in the 'top-down approach', which is very common in the heritage and museum sector, all decisions are made using only 'expert knowledge', which neglects community dynamics, needs and priorities as well as diverse backgrounds. Although the latter has been considered an issue in last couple of decades and museums and heritage platforms have begun to pay more attention to people rather than object-based projects in Europe, the United Kingdom and the USA (see Simon 2010; Sandell and Nightingle 2012; Chynoweth et al. 2020), the structural inequality and injustices still can be seen widely in top-down museum and heritage work worldwide. The main difference between the top-down approach and the people-centred approach is around creating knowledge. Local knowledge is created on the ground through the relationships of community members in the social and cultural life with various dynamics. On the contrary, top-down knowledge is created without knowing the dynamics of social and cultural life of local communities, and because of this, experts impose their own agendas.

The top-down approach or expert knowledge-based practice (see Schofield 2016) brings many ethical issues in the heritage and museum contexts. One pitfall of top-down approach is that it only aims to 'transfer knowledge' to their audiences without creating opportunities and platforms to critically engage, question and use the knowledge that's gained from the material culture for community skills development. In the words of Paulo Freire (1970), audiences are considered 'objects' whose role is only to receive knowledge without questioning or interrogating it. Additionally, the lack of attention to community cohesion, needs and priorities and diverse forms of community identities, including ethnicity, class, sex and race, is still a big issue in the heritage and museum sector worldwide. The heritage and museum projects' content that is designed to be circulated to different age groups could be more critical and constructivist, more linked to the social, cultural, economic and political lives of individuals and more focused on supporting disadvantaged groups. The content especially needs to consider the backgrounds of individuals and groups whose identity construction has a great influence on how these individuals and groups engage with and interpret material culture.

2.1 Approaches and Methods

Approaches and methods in museum and heritage practices are progressing and shifting substantially. These changes affect, in particular, the traditional idea of the role of museums and heritage that was used to consolidate nation states and ideologies as well as to consume people's material culture as part of the colonial approach. The shift can particularly be seen in heritage sites and museums' public engagement projects where heritage sites and museums are now more often considered not only as places where objects are preserved but also as spaces for people in particular. Many national and international heritage and museum institutions and associations are recognising the importance of the educational role of museums and heritage sites and this is reflected in policy documents and education campaigns. One example is the 'museums change lives' campaign carried out by the Museum Association in the United Kingdom,[5] which focused on the educational role of museums. Similarly in the USA, the American Associations of Museums[6] has long recognised the need for diversity in heritage and museum work. The latter specifically emphasised 'critical thinking, contemplation and dialogue'. Furthermore, UNESCO[7] made educational activities one of their essential criteria as part of the management plans for becoming a World Heritage Site.

Despite education being recognised as a fundamental tool that should have a critical, constructive and diverse approach, the top-down design of education programmes that only transfer and impose knowledge without a critical approach dealing with inequalities is still common in many museums and heritage sites across the world. This approach, of course, has its own dynamics in countries where museums and heritage sites are controlled by a state's central government that doesn't allow for diverse interpretations of the material culture but rather imposes a single interpretation that is in line with the state's ideology. While this happens in Turkey (Apaydin 2016c) or in China (see Zhang 2020), for instance, diverse interpretations of material culture can also be enabled; however, this happens through private museums (those not controlled by the state) or through grassroots heritage movements, such as the Gezi Park protests in 2013 in Turkey (Apaydin 2020b). However, developing different, critical and constructivist approaches and methods, which consider the audiences' profiles, needs and priorities, have also been neglected in many other museums and heritage sites. This neglect further led to a 'global template' for education programmes in which the same approach and methods have been used in many parts of the world in heritage and museum contexts.

One of the greatest pitfalls in using the 'global template', which I will delve into below, is that it neglects the locality that is developed through the

---

[5] See www.museumsassociation.org/campaigns/museums-change-lives/.

[6] See www.aam-us.org/wp-content/uploads/2017/12/Demographic-Change-and-the-Future-of-Museums.pdf.

[7] See https://whc.unesco.org/en/documents/?action=list&category=management_plans.

interaction of people and nature or people and material culture, which also creates local values. Particularly, within the framework of global template of education programmes, the main principles of critical theories and social justice approaches have been widely neglected despite the fact that educational theories are common and well developed in other fields of humanities. One of the most popular learning theories that is used in the heritage and museum context is 'experiential learning theory', developed by David Kolb (1984) and later adopted into 'interactive' or 'contextual learning' by Falk and Dierking (2018). Experiential learning theory is based on the process of experience and individual's or participant's reflection in the learning process. It focuses on the participant's cognitive processes and it is a cycle that has different stages: 'active experimentation, concrete experience, reflective observation and abstract conceptualising' (Kolb 1984). Similarly, 'the contextual model' places learning in real settings and emphasises "the personal context, the sociocultural context, and the physical context" and Falk and Dierking argue that "learning is the process/product of the interactions between these three contexts" (2018, 7). Both learning theories have their own merits and are applied widely in a range of cultural settings in heritage sites and museum settings as part of a global template for education programmes. One of the most common ways of utilising these learning theories in archaeology, museum and heritage contexts include hands-on experiences, making replicas of objects and artefacts and, especially in archaeology contexts, involving communities and creating artificial spaces for schoolchildren to 'dig out' artefacts (see Young Archaeologist Club; Museum of London education programmes; British Museum[8]). These educational methods are now also quite common across the world (see Çakir Ilhan 2009 for Turkey; Hein 2012 for USA; Lang and Reeve 2018 for Asia).

These learning theories and the interactive activities they have inspired, of course, have value and help to develop awareness through the preserving material culture and heritage as well as contributing greatly to heritage sites and museums. However, my questions are: how can these theories and methods be further developed in theory and praxis to help to address the inequalities in our society from an educational perspective? I argue that the role of heritage and museum education shouldn't only be about preserving material culture or learning about the past but that it should be used as a tool to challenge contemporary issues. The protection and preservation of the past material culture are, of course, important but this is not the priority of people whose needs and demands are different from the protection of material culture in most

[8] See www.yac-uk.org/things-to-do; www.museumoflondon.org.uk/schools/interactive-sessions; www.britishmuseum.org/learn/schools.

cases. A recent worldwide survey[9] conducted by UNESCO shows that people consider that 'climate change and loss of biodiversity' are the biggest issues, followed by 'violence and conflict', 'discrimination and inequality' and 'lack of food, water and housing'. So how do current heritage practices and education programmes, both in heritage sites and museums, respond to these issues? Or do they respond at all? To answer this question, in Sections 2.2, 2.3, 2.4 and 2.5, I will examine heritage and museum practices with case studies and different approaches that I divide into authoritarian, global, creative and critical and digital practices.

2.2 Authoritarian Practices

Since the 1980s, when neoliberalism and its associated policies began to impact our lives, particularly through marketisation and consumerism, heritage sites and museums also became important places because there was a high correlation with marketisation, profit-making and 'consuming' one's culture (see Silberman 2007). While democratic economies used this as an opportunity to make more profit (Hewison 1987), neoliberalism also fuelled undemocratic and authoritarian regimes (Brown 2019) that eliminated, neglected and consumed, especially, minority ethnic groups' heritage by denying their identity and material culture (Apaydin 2018). Turkey is one of those countries, among many, that has become undemocratic and authoritarian, especially in last decade, and 'under the idea of economic development' (see Brown 2019), minority ethnic group heritage has been used to make a profit (Apaydin 2016a) and through large infrastructure projects, such as dam building, minority ethnic group heritage has been destroyed (see Apaydin 2020b). However, although this is strongly linked to neoliberal policies, it is also linked to the one nation, one state idea that oppresses minority ethnic groups and their heritage. Whilst the idea of a one nation state and neoliberalism can be considered two different concepts, neoliberalism is an effective method to eliminate minority ethnic group heritage, landscape and identity that are often considered threats to national unity in undemocratic nation states. For instance, Turkey has used neoliberalism, under the gloss of economic development, in Kurdish regions where large dams have been constructed to wipe out the landscape of the region where memories are developed, identities constructed and values attached (see Ronayne 2005). The construction of dam projects resulted in destroying Kurdish heritage and identity and at the same time, made a profit for the state.

---

[9] See https://en.unesco.org/news/unesco-world-2030-survey-report-highlights-youth-concerns-over-climate-change-and-biodiversity.

Despite Turkey's very multicultural history, with Armenians, Kurds, Alevis and Greeks and many more, this culturally diverse past and material culture don't get the attention they deserve in displays and education programmes of museums. Except for very rare examples, the focus is more or less on the Ottoman, Islamic and Turkish heritage, in line with the Turkish official ideology (see Zencirci 2014) or the prehistoric past and archaeological heritage. It is important to point out that museums and heritage sites in Turkey are centrally controlled – except for private museums – and policies and decisions are taken by the Ministry of Culture and Tourism (see Baraldi et al. 2013) and implemented at the local level without any community consultation. This strict centralised control also affects museum displays and education programmes, which are designed and presented in line with the national identity, based on 'Turkishness', and to make more profit where it is possible. Museum displays, in line with the state and government ideology, can be seen in many museums in Turkey now, for instance at the 'Topkapi Palace Museum', where the current ruling party, the Justice and Development Party's new ideology of 'new Turkey', based on Ottoman values, can clearly be seen (Kınıkoğlu 2021). Similarly, 'The Panorama 1453 Historical Museum', which was established in 2009 and focuses on conquering Istanbul from the Byzantine Empire, is another example where the 'new Turkey' ideology is imposed (Posocco 2018). This type of imposition on cultural settings is strongly linked to the developing and preserving of ideology or to conserve the idea of the one nation, one state, as in the case of Turkey. This is also one of the other main reasons that heritage sites and state museums are centrally controlled in Turkey. In this strictly controlled and authoritarian structure, all interpretation of displays and education programmes are designed through a top-down approach without critical reflections on history and the past and contemporary social and political issues, with a strong exclusion of community stakeholders.

For example, consider the Archaeology Museum in Kars, in eastern Turkey.[10] This region used to be very multicultural, with different cultural identities and ethnic groups but mainly Armenian. Although the museum displays a selection of artefacts from different parts of the region, the most significant displays come from the heritage site of Ani, whose monumental heritage was built by Armenians during the medieval period (see Apaydin 2018). During my ethnographic fieldwork seasons at Ani, I met many Armenians from the diaspora who live in the USA and across Europe but come to visit the site as it is still significant for their cultural memory. However, the museum's displays, interpretations and education programmes don't reflect on the history of Armenian

---

[10] See www.kulturportali.gov.tr/turkiye/kars/gezilecekyer/kars-muzesi.

people who attached meanings, developed memories and values and constructed their identities in the past in this region. Similarly, eastern and southeastern Turkey are also home to the Kurds, who have lived there for generations and used the landscape and nature to develop a sense of place and sense of community (see Ronayne 2005). However, none of the state museums in the region reflects on the history, the past and material culture of the Kurds in their displays or education programmes – the Kurdish identity is not recognised at any level (see Girard 2015) as Kurdish people are considered as a threat to the one–nation state ideology (see Watts 2010).

A similar approach can also be seen with Greek heritage, especially in western Turkey, which was home to millions of Greeks until the 1920s (see Akdar 2000). Despite the fact that western Turkey has many archaeological museums containing objects and artefacts from ancient and recent Greek culture, Greek heritage (especially modern Greek heritage) gets little attention in displays and educational activities that are run by the museums.[11] Although most museums and heritage specialists recognise the multicultural past and the material culture of Greeks and other minority groups, this isn't reflected in the museums because the state doesn't allow the democratic, critical and diverse designs for museum displays and education programmes.

This lack of reflecting other cultures and histories in museums is strongly linked to the construction of modern Turkey's one nation, one state policy, which focuses on a single ethnicity. This policy led to the 'purification' process in the first half of the twentieth century and has continued to the modern day through methods such as misrecognising and neglecting minority group heritage at the museums or in formal education (see Apaydin 2016c). This is, of course, state-endorsed heritage presentation in the cultural and public settings. In contrast to the state-oriented heritage presentations and displays, there are heritage NGOs that act as grassroots heritage organisations to bring the multicultural heritage to public attention. For instance, *Anadolu Kültür*,[12] a non-profit heritage and art organisation, organised educational and art events and exhibitions across Turkey to emphasise and highlight the multicultural past of Turkey and to build bridges between diverse communities and initiate dialogues.

In addition to the Turkish state deliberately neglecting and misrecognising minority groups' material culture (also see Apaydin 2018) in museums and heritage sites, the state has also promoted particular heritage sites in order to obtain UNESCO World Heritage Site status. For instance, the site of Ani, which

---

[11] See Ephesus Museum https://muze.gov.tr/muze-detay?SectionId=EFM01&DistId=EFM and Izmir Archaeology Museum https://muze.gov.tr/muze-detay?DistId=MRK&SectionId=IZA01.

[12] See www.anadolukultur.org/EN/.

is a monumental Armenian heritage site, became a World Heritage Site in 2016.[13] However, the Armenians' existence, heritage and past were not given the same attention as the Turkish and Ottoman heritage at Ani, despite the fact that millions of Armenians lived in Turkey and left architectural and monumental heritage all across Turkey.[14] Ani never lost its importance for Armenians because it represents their identity, their sense of belonging and tangible imbued memories (Apaydin 2018). The site is also important for the Turks who see the conquest of the site by Seljuks in 1041 as the beginning of the arrival of Turks to Anatolia and this is what is promoted by the state. Ani illustrates how heritage sites can be contentious because the Turkish state doesn't recognise Armenians' existence at the site: the word 'Armenian' was never included on the site entrance panel before UNESCO inscription, similarly to Kars Archaeology Museum. As another example: the famous cathedral at Ani was built during the Armenian Kingdom period and was later turned into a mosque. The information panel doesn't mention the word Armenian at all (see Figure 1). This demonstrates how the authoritarian understanding of the past or, in other words, acknowledging only one single side of history is a threat to minority groups. Chimamanda Ngozi Adichie argues that this kind of single-sided approach has 'the danger' because its intent is to suppress other groups of people (2009, 01:43), which is consistent with Young's concept of oppression.

Young's (1990, 48) five faces of oppression, 'exploitation, marginalisation, powerlessness, cultural imperialism and violence', fit well with this kind of top-down and authoritarian design of heritage and museum practice in Turkey.

Exploitation. Although Young's 'exploitation' form of oppression is linked directly to the injustice of class division between labourer and owner, which increases inequality, exploitation can also be seen in the case of the abuse of Armenian and Kurdish heritage because they are not recognised in cultural settings but their heritage and landscapes are used for profit making by Turkish elite classes, who also have the power of control.

Marginalisation. Young points out that marginalisation is one of the most dangerous forms of oppression and excludes individuals and groups from social and cultural life and even further, it leads to the loss of community identity and its extermination. She particularly points out "the material deprivation marginalization often causes is certainly unjust, especially in a society where others have plenty" (1990, 53). Considering the Armenians in Turkey, who were subjected to genocide and ethnic cleansing in the past (Akçam 2004), and later, their identity was neglected and misrecognised in every part of state institution, including education as well as museums, they've lost their sense

---

[13] See https://whc.unesco.org/en/list/1518/.
[14] See https://turkiyekulturvarliklari.hrantdink.org/?lang=en.

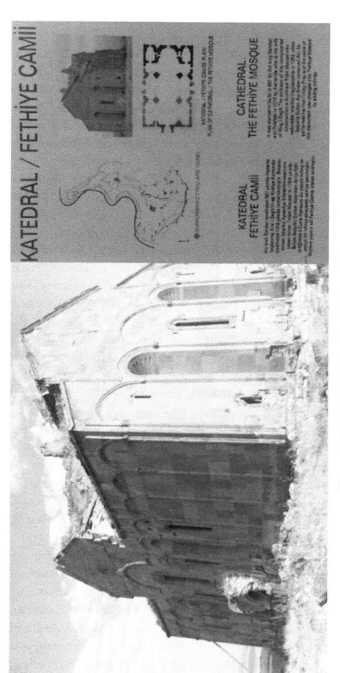

Figure 1 Cathedral at Ani and public description panel

of community and place that bound their collective identity together. Thus, most Armenians migrated and sought refuge in other parts of the world, especially in Europe and the USA.

Powerlessness. As I discussed earlier, I consider heritage settings, including sites and museums, as spaces for communities to use for social production. At this point, *powerlessness* is directly linked to exploitation and marginality. Powerlessness represents the people whose labour is not recognised but is consumed by the class who has the power, as in the case of Armenians and Kurds, whose cultural, social and economic labour that produced heritage over centuries is being consumed by the Turkish elites who hold the power.

Cultural imperialism. The material culture is perhaps the most directly linked cultural imperialism form of oppression. Young (1990, 59) points out that "cultural imperialism consists in the universalisation of one group's experience and culture, and its establishment as the norm" (also see Said 1994 on 'culture and imperialism'). This is more dependent on access to 'capital' because some groups have more access than others in different parts of society and some groups have control of the 'interpretation and communication' in a society (also see Fraser 1987). In other words, because of access inequality and a single group's dominance in terms of using communication tools in a society, the dominant group's cultural products are more widely disseminated, with their values and meanings, and as it becomes more dominant, it undermines other groups who don't have access to communication tools. The social, cultural and economic life contexts and heritage sites and museums in Turkey provide an example of this.

As I pointed out earlier, heritage sites and museums in Turkey are dominated by an elite class who hold the power and therefore all communication tools as well. This widely impacts the display of the material culture in the museums and the care of heritage sites that are linked to Turkishness or, in other words, that are used to prove ownership rights of the lands against minority groups, such as the Armenians and Kurds. This nationalist approach that has been implemented by elites of Turkey goes back to the 1920s when Turkey was established. Research projects were held in the first couple of decades of the new Republic to form all communication tools, such as formal education, from the Turkish nationalism perspective. For instance, some archaeological sites were excavated that were thought could be linked to Turkish ethnicity and nationalism (see Atakuman 2008). Congresses and conferences were held, such as the 'Turkish Historical Thesis' congress and the 'Turkish Review of Anthropology' to prove that the land of Turkey had always been Turkish. This approach continues today, especially in informal and formal education contexts. The knowledge of the products of Turkish culture is used to assimilate and further eliminate minority groups and different cultural identity groups in Turkey by imposing a 'legitimate' knowledge that denies the multicultural past of Turkey and only recognises and promotes Turkish ethnicity (see Apaydin 2018). However, since Turkey has been undergoing a transformation under an authoritarian government led by the Justice and Development Party (JDP), whose ideology is based on Islam and Ottomanism, it is important to differentiate existing uses of heritage and museums by elites. Since 2002, when the JDP came to power, they have also created their own elites who control the social, cultural and economic resources, including state-run museums and cultural settings that reflect the ideology of 'new Turkey'. On the other hand, small, private museums owned by the elites of secular Turkey also still exist. These small museums occasionally present and display the multicultural heritage of Turkey, for instance, the Museum of Innocence[15] and Sakip Sabanci Museum,[16] and a couple of museums that are directly linked to minorities such as the Jewish Museum[17] in Istanbul.

Violence. The form of violence as part of oppression more or less affects many groups who are not from the dominant culture. Young (1990) exemplifies this with the USA. As she points out, violence occurs systematically and it is 'legitimate' and this can be seen, for example, in all discriminated groups (including people of colour, indigenous people, the LGBTQ+ community and others). Similar violence in the past and present has been seen in Turkey in the case of the Kurdish and Armenian communities. This is also linked to the 'cultural imperialism' form, and the dominant groups in the society, especially in the education context (formal and informal), prevent people from learning about minority cultures through the material culture that is displayed in museums, and this leads to racism, prejudice and even violence.

2.3 Global Practices

Heritage and museum education programmes have become very popular and have been used as an outreach tool in many museums in most parts of the world. The same approach and methods are universally applied in many parts of the world. I call this type of programme 'global template education programmes'. Most of these education programmes do not consider community dynamics, priorities, needs and diversities as part of their top-down approaches. They are not based on the individual community's own values, developed through the interaction of individuals and groups with their environment and landscape, creating 'locality' and local values (Appadurai 1995). Every community and culture has its own dynamics and community cohesion, and they have different

---

[15] See https://artsandculture.google.com/story/KAVxIqBekvaEKw?hl=en.
[16] See www.sakipsabancimuzesi.org/en.   [17] See www.muze500.com/index.php?lang=en.

priorities and needs (Cohen 1985) that should be considered when developing education programmes, and museums especially need to reflect on this important aspect in practice. The difference in community cohesion also reflects on the interpretation of material culture from one community to another. Most importantly, using the same approach and method neglects the reflection of inequalities and injustices and it doesn't challenge the social, political and economic issues. This brings us to the question of 'What are heritage sites and museums for?'

In Turkey, in addition to the authoritarian practices of heritage and museums, heritage education that is run by heritage sites or museums controlled by the central government or private museums is very common (see Çakir Ilhan 2009). The approach of experiential and contextual learning is applied well with methods (hands-on experiences, creating replicas of objects), similar to practices in other parts of the world. For example, the Çatalhöyük Museum centre's education programme was one of those where the experiential practice was seen clearly and I had a chance to evaluate and assess this education programme (Figure 2). Çatalhöyük is a well-researched Neolithic site located in Turkey and attained UNESCO World Heritage Site status in 2012[18] (Figure 3). The site's archaeological research history goes back to the 1960s but it was researched with one of the most interdisciplinary and international teams between 1994 and 2016. It was also one of the rare heritage projects with a multidisciplinary approach in education, exhibitions and public engagement activities.

The education programme at Çatalhöyük was one of the world's longest-running heritage site-based education programmes that aimed to increase 'protection of cultural heritage', and ran from 2002 to 2015.[19] The programme was developed and run using the 'top-down' approach by archaeologists and educators, who also used strong experiential and contextual learning theories to engage participants in different age groups from eight to fourteen. Approximately five thousand students attended these programmes over the years. A typical education day at the museum involved an introductory lecture about Çatalhöyük, followed by a site visit and then a workshop where students could make replicas of the artefacts or Neolithic art paintings. After conducting archival research, I managed to locate thirty students who attended these education programmes several years previously. The aim of my evaluation was to measure the impact of the museum centre education programmes. To do this, I also located another thirty students as a 'control group' – these students were local people and the same age as the experiential group but never attended these education programmes. I used

---

[18] See https://whc.unesco.org/en/list/1405/.
[19] See www.catalhoyuk.com/archive_reports/2015.

Figure 2 Çatalhöyük Museum Centre's education programme. Participants are participating in a hands-on experience

questionnaires to see if and how these education programmes impacted on the participants' perceptions, skills and knowledge. The result of questionnaires from both groups indicated that there was not much difference between the two groups, showing the ineffectiveness of this education programme. The most striking pitfall of this education programme was the neglect of the most important question, 'How can the past material culture and prehistory provide the ground-work to deal with and challenge the issues that the world is having today?'

In the case of Çatalhöyük, as a Neolithic society, one of its most interesting and powerful features, based on archaeological evidence, was its egalitarian socio-political structure (see Hodder and Marciniak 2015). Archaeological research indicates that people lived a non-hierarchical lifestyle, had equal access to resources and had 'non-biological social bonds' that tied community members together. Very importantly, it was a non-violent society. The case of Çatalhöyük not only demonstrates how the past material culture has the poten-tial to start a dialogue with the contemporary people who may be able to

Figure 3 Overview of Çatalhöyük, UNESCO World Heritage Site

critically think and explore possibilities of an equal, non-discriminative and non-violent future (see Borck 2019) but also, it shows us that alternative ways of living existed in the past and, therefore, alternative futures and different world histories can be created, as Graeber and Wengrow (2021) point out. Although the scientific evidence clearly shows that the Neolithic community of Çatalhöyük had very egalitarian lifestyle, with no evidence of violence and gender discrimination, which could be used to demonstrate that the past material culture can be a main driver in thinking critically and challenging social, political, economic issues including racism, prejudice, discrimination, sexual discrimination and poverty, these important aspects were totally neglected in the Çatalhöyük museum centre education. A similar neglect can also be seen in the display and education programmes of the Museum of Anatolian Civilizations in Ankara, which displays Çatalhöyük archaeological objects. The museum does not employ a critical and constructivist approach in engaging audiences through displays and education programmes and further, the displays only focus on the date, the material of objects and what was it used for. The pitfalls of using the same approach and the methods that lead to the ineffectiveness of museum engagement can also be seen in the well-known museums in the other parts of Europe and the world as well. Similar approaches and methods can be seen in most museums in Turkey (see Çakir Ilhan 2009) that are based on transferring knowledge rather than engaging audiences critically.

This type of traditional approach and method is certainly important from the perspective of community engagement and especially developing awareness among young people for the protection of material culture and recognising the importance of archaeology. However, these programmes could also reflect on, for example, why archaeology is a crucial field to learn about the past and contemplate and offer platforms to discuss social and political issues in the world today, and, most importantly, why engaging with archaeology and material culture is important, especially from the point of developing 'historical empathy'.

Historical empathy features three important components (see Endacott and Brooks 2013), especially the importance of the material culture of the past and present. *Historical contextualisation* reflects on the understanding of historical facts and makes a connection between the past and present. *Perspective taking* creates consciousness and understanding of alternative beliefs and values, the recognition of alternative contexts and it leads to rethinking pre-existing ideas and perspectives. *Affective connection* is more about developing emotional responses to past cultures through the material culture (see McKinney 2018 for more details). In other words, material culture, as it is tangible, has great potential to make 'contact' between people and other cultures in the sense of alternative ways of life because material culture or object has the power as they store meanings, values and memories of people. In *The Comfort of Things* (2009), Danial Miller carried out an extensive anthropological study on 'things' or objects that people use by examining thirty households in London and exposed the importance and value of daily objects that people use to make their life meaningful.

Material culture is developed through people who ascribe meanings, develop memories and values and construct their identities. Therefore, it is the most significant and crucial symbol of cultural representation and has the potential to introduce particular cultures and has the potential to develop critical consciousness to start a dialogue between cultures and communities. In other words, by experiencing different forms of material culture, visitors or participants in such sites are exposed to alternative ideas and ways of thinking (both of other cultures and forms of the past). This in turn helps to provide the groundwork to prevent discrimination, racism and prejudice that we face in everyday life. Heritage sites and museums as social spaces where knowledge is produced and redistributed should be able to respond to contemporary issues as well as historical problems. As I pointed out earlier, this is strongly linked to the approach and methods that are being taken by heritage and museum institutions.

Consider the British Museum, with its wide collections that reflect on diversity of the world's historic and contemporary cultures with its permanent and temporary exhibitions. My MA students and I carry out workshops at the British Museum and evaluate their educational programmes every year. It has systematic in-person and online education programmes that include digital media tools for schools and different age groups from Key Stage 2 to Key Stage 5 (ages seven to eighteen). Most of the collections that are on display are interpreted and designed through top-down approaches and with expert knowledge. This top-down approach also strongly reflects on the design of education programmes that neglects multivocality and collaborative design, which has potential to bring different and diverse voices for interpretation of material culture.

The education programmes apply strong 'experiential and contextual learning' theories in their learning programmes as they are designed and based on interactive and hands-on learning through digital tools or replicas of objects. The content of the education programmes, both in virtual and in-person learning, are incredibly rich and represent the museum's worldwide collections. However, several issues arise from these learning programmes from the justice and equality perspective. First, despite these programmes being designed by considering different school age groups, the content of learning programmes neglects the diversity theme through the material culture and is far from developing historical empathy which, I argue, is one of the other most important components through learning material culture, especially in the archaeology context. Developing historical empathy is not only important for critical learning programmes but also has the great potential to reduce injustices that are especially embedded in racial and cultural discrimination in today's world, as I discussed in the case of Çatalhöyük.

Considering different themes of British museum's learning programmes, for instance, the 'Roman Britain treasure challenge' that brings insight from this period of Britain but doesn't reflect on how this period was culturally diverse, or the 'Indus Valley investigation' and 'Ancient Egypt' learning programmes that only reflect on objects but don't touch on alternative beliefs and values that existed in the past that would lead to the development of historical empathy. For instance, the Assyrian collection of the British Museum could be used to develop empathy towards Syrian refugees and preserve their sense of identity and sense of community.

Heritage sites and museums are learning spaces where individuals and groups interact with material culture of the past and contemporary cultures. This approach has been dealt with worldwide heritage and museum practices by offering a range of learning activities online or offline as in the case of the British Museum. One of the pitfalls of taking a top-down approach is that it limits the collaboration and excludes people from the design and inter-pretation of material culture. London is one of the most multicultural cities in the world and the British Museum has worldwide collections from the past and contemporary cultures. Taking a people-centred approach by including people in the design and interpretation process would allow not only ethical and diverse voices but also have the potential to lead to reducing inequalities and injustices as the museum can create space for those communities to have a voice in decision-making processes, as the British Museum does indeed do in some of its projects (see next section). At this point, the role of museums should also be considered as public institutions that should not only encourage communities to take a role in this process but act on this, because design and delivery of heritage work cannot be done without strong public collaboration.

2.4 Creative and Critical Practices

As opposed to the top-down approach and authoritarian practices discussed previously, which avoid criticality and diverse voices and identities in heritage sites and museums, we have also seen unique, critical and creative practices and education designs. These practices instead aim to reflect on difficult histories and heritage, injustices and inequalities as well as to emphasise the importance of differences in community in terms of identity, gender, class and social and economic backgrounds, through engaging with diverse communities. For example, the British Museum's recent work on 'object journeys',[20] which aims at developing an approach for UK museums with the collaboration of communities to research, interpret and display collections, is a great example that demonstrates a collaborative approach. As part of this programme, 'the Somali Object Journeys' and 'Kribati Object Journeys' (Figures 4 and 5) were collaborations with communities of Somali and Kiribati heritage in London, who researched and interpreted collections from their own cultures at the museum. While this type of people-centred approach overcomes many ethical issues and reduces top-down design and interpretation of cultural objects, it also provides the groundwork for disadvantaged groups to take part in decision-making processes and, most importantly, enables them to develop 'cultural capital' and skills by taking part in cultural spaces. This approach gives these groups the opportunities to manage and introduce their own culture to different audiences through material culture, thus audiences have direct contact with these cultures. This type of people-centred approach is also necessary to develop content and to deliver education programmes to develop critical

---

[20] See www.britishmuseum.org/learn/communities/projects.

Figure 4 Somali Object Journey's display at the British Museum

dialogues as part of a democratic approach. However, while I point out critical impacts and potentials of these projects to overcome many issues, these projects also have great potential to end up replicating the museum's own exhibitions although communities are included in those projects. In other words, the curator of the institutions implements their own agendas in the end and communities become a tick box for future funding applications. Additionally, these kinds of critical and inclusive projects are also often used to cover bigger institutional issues, for instance, repatriation and restitution issues (see Joy 2020), therefore it is not only important to shift approaches and methods, but it is also necessary for many institutions to go through institutional transformation (see Ahmed 2012). To avoid these problems, it is important to look at Freire's models for content development and building dialogue for educational settings and con-textualise them in heritage and museum settings. I will get back to this in more detail in Section 3.

These types of community-based approaches can be seen in some other, small museums in the United Kingdom. Hackney Museum[21] in northeast London, is

---
[21] See https://hackney-museum.hackney.gov.uk/.

Figure 5 A participant of Somali Object Journey's working on an object at the British Museum

one museum that offers diverse learning programmes. The museum, with its permanent and temporary exhibitions, also reflects well on the diverse histories of the neighbourhood. This includes finds from recent archaeological excavations and finds from the archaeological projects in the Olympic area, linked to the migration to Hackney from different parts of the world. The exhibitions of Hackney Museum present a tangible and intangible heritage of its communities who migrated to Hackney. This diverse and inclusive exhibiting of community histories through the material culture and storytelling are also reflected in Hackney Museum's educational resources and programmes[22] (Figures 6, 7, 8, 9).

---

[22] See https://hackney-museum.hackney.gov.uk/learning/.

Figure 6 A panel display with description of the Olympic Park excavations and
archaeological finds at Hackney Museum

The museum offers different learning programmes for different age groups.
The design of the programmes was created taking into consideration the different learning abilities of people who have different backgrounds. The museum
works with school teachers and considers the English National Curriculum
when designing the content of their learning programmes. The learning

Figure 7 Story of Blanca who came to Hackney from Austria on the Kindertransport

programmes include very critical content because they reflect on difficult histories and heritage, such as migration and socio-political issues in the neighbourhood: 'Hackney history at home: refugee week 2020', 'How diaries can capture history' and 'Collecting your family's story' – all of which reflect on the different heritages and histories of Hackney as well as on learning about recent community developments.

The design and content of Hackney Museum's education programmes and resources are crucially important in two ways. First, Hackney Museum offers its audiences the opportunity to learn about the diverse cultural construction of this particular neighbourhood and to learn about other cultures. Learning about other cultures, directly or through material culture and intangible assets, is important in order to develop empathy and prevent biases, prejudices and racism, as psychologist Gordon Allport (1954) pointed out in his 'contact theory', which is still widely used in psychological studies, and it is significant for creating contact zones in museum contexts (Clifford 1997; for more on 'contact theory' and 'contact zone', see Section 3).

Figure 8 Story of Mohamed who came to Hackney as a child from Sierra Leone during the war

Second, while Hackney Museum reflects widely and elaborately on the history of the region, from archaeological artefacts to recent history, it also offers platforms to learn about the diverse histories as well as challenging historical issues, which is perhaps one of the most important principles of museums in theory (see Kidd et al. 2017). One example is an educational resource of 'African and Caribbean history and heritage in Hackney' that includes 'Black British history' linked to Hackney from 400 years ago up to today with images, films, personal stories and exhibitions. While this learning resource is important from the perspective of demonstrating to students that different cultural groups have lived together for centuries in Hackney, constructing and sharing history and the past, it is also significant for the African

Figure 9 Mary Meade – Victorian suitcase. Represents the life of a maid during the Victorian period

and Caribbean community in terms of recognition of their heritage and the past. This is important as the activities and programmes of Hackney Museum are very much linked to the Black Lives Matter (BLM) movement, which became a mainstream social justice movement.

Similar creative and critical approaches can also be seen in the practices of the Museum of the Home[23] and Sutton House[24] also located in this part of northeast London. At these institutions, the focus shifted towards diverse practices and education programmes where historical and contemporary issues are placed in the content and exhibitions. Although these three museums are small neighbourhood museums, with limited funding and with limited resources and staff members, it shows how museums should act when considering their social, cultural and political roles in the twenty-first century to develop sustainable future communities. However, other museums that have better or more

---

[23] See www.museumofthehome.org.uk/learning/communities/.

[24] See www.nationaltrust.org.uk/sutton-house-and-breakers-yard/primary-learning.

resources can engage with different audiences and redistribute the knowledge of material culture and intangible heritage more effectively through more creative and critical approaches.

Although heritage education is common for heritage sites as mentioned in the previous section, most of them are far from being critical and creative, so participants are not able to engage with inequalities and injustices or social, political and economic issues of the world today. This is important from a critical perspective as heritage practices have the potential to develop 'critical consciousness' and 'counter-narratives' that participants can engage in to make changes. In our Emotive project,[25] which was funded by the European Commission, we conducted alternative research that included a different approach and method to Çatalhöyük museum centre's education programme (discussed in the previous section).

In the Emotive project, we developed a digital education kit.[26] The content of the education kit, which included apps and a chatbot, was developed after considering, for example, the Turkish formal education context that neglects the prehistoric past and heritages mentioned above ('authoritarian practices'). The focus of the kit was to explore egalitarianism from a critical perspective and to lead participants to explore and question their past lives, link to their own lives and to critically think about alternative ways of living in the future through using the Exploration of Egalitarianism Kit (Figure 10). Based on the archaeo-logical evidence, the society of Çatalhöyük lived a very egalitarian life that didn't have social stratification, everyone was equal and food was distributed equally (see Hodder and Marciniak 2015). Our role as researchers was not to direct or tell participants how to reinterpret archaeology and heritage but instead to facilitate their ability to think in more critical ways about what the past might have been like and what directions are possible for future society. This approach we applied is exactly opposed to mainstream formal and informal education models as well as the 'banking education model' that was outlined and dis-cussed by Paul Freire, who emphasises that in this model students are receiving the knowledge as it is imposed to them by the teachers without critical thinking and questioning.

The education kit was designed to reflect on these important aspects and led participants to compare this egalitarian past life and their current lives and community. It encouraged participants to learn more about and experience this alternative life by letting participants manage these digital tools to learn more and question contemporary inequalities and injustices. Following this

---

[25] See https://emotiveproject.eu/.

[26] See http://athena.emotiveproject.eu/schoolkit/UsingtheKit.html.

Figure 10 Emotive project at Çatalhöyük. Participants are experiencing an
egalitarian lifestyle through digital media tools

forty-minute experience, we conducted a post-experience survey and interview
with each participant and followed up with questionnaires to be collected
several days later to see the impact of the experience. Most of the participants,
during the interview, reflected on the egalitarian lifestyle very critically and
compared their current life under post capitalism; participants questioned modern life and pointed out injustices in terms of economic wealth distribution,
inequality in society, discrimination against other groups and reflected strongly
on gender differences. For instance, some of the participants reflected on
'sharing' and 'peace' concepts by comparing today and the Neolithic world:

> ... When we consider today's society, it is full of people who don't help each
> other but here [at Neolithic Çatalhöyük society] they figured out how to help
> each other without and education ... I mean we have too many [economic]
> classes today. For example, there are many rich and poor ... I think every-
> thing is possible through good education, the differences can be minimised.

> ... I would want this kind of change [in the community] ... in the past, people were very close and sharing, friendship e.g., were important ... these were making peace in the community but today, everybody is selfish and there is no peace in the community .... I would have preferred a community like Çatalhöyük.

The experience of Emotive didn't only just provide different interpretations of the past, but it also offered opportunities and created the groundwork for participants to engage with the past from different perspectives by allowing them to bring their own life experiences and locality into the interpretation. This kind of people-centred action research is also significant in closing the gap developed through formal education.

2.5 Digital Practices

The development in the use of technology has greatly impacted heritage practices in sites and museums, and various digital media tools have been developed and used to present heritage and engage with different audiences to increase participation in heritage. This development also changed the ways of presenting collections in museums in the last couple of decades (see Kidd 2014; Drotner et al. 2018). The wide range of digital media tools (websites, apps, virtual tours, mainly offsite media) has become popular and commonplace. The COVID-19 pandemic also demonstrated the importance of digital media to engage with audiences during the lockdown. Digital media is, of course, also important for redistributing the knowledge of museums and heritage sites to wider audiences. However, two crucial issues have been neglected, undermining the use of digital media to reach wider audiences in heritage sites and museums.

First, as in the case of most global heritage and museum practices as I discussed in Section 2.3, most digital media platforms are designed from a top-down perspective as users don't have opportunity to contribute to the design of these experiences. Rather, they only receive the knowledge that's implemented from these sites and digital platforms, though there are emerging methods that enable users to contribute (see Tallon and Walker 2008). In contrast, alternative and more egalitarian forms of digital engagement can offer numerous opportunities to decolonise knowledge and reflect on socio-cultural and political issues, if it is designed from a critical perspective that leads participants to make their own understanding from the digital collections. This also has the potential to increase the participation of collaborative engagement at museums and heritage sites. Deuze (2006, 66) points out that digital media is an "active agent in the process of meaning making because we adopt but at the same time modify, manipulate, and this reform consensual ways of understanding reality and we reflexively assemble our own particular versions of such reality". This is also true from the perspective of the use of social media platforms that people use for daily life and create meanings. For instance, 'Douyin', a Chinese social media platform, is used for daily purposes and as an active agent for people's communication and learning. This not only deconstructs institutional power and censorship but it also gives people power to control knowledge.

Second, and perhaps most importantly, is the digital access issue: do digital media increase inequalities among socially, culturally and economically different groups in society? Although the use of digital media is significant because it offers skills development, it also creates a large gap for many disadvantaged groups who don't have access or the skills to use these digital media platforms that have been developed by museums and galleries. This is also linked to Bourdieu's theory of cultural capital as groups who already have access to a good education are also able to further develop their skills further through using digital media tools as they already have the base skills (see Bennett et al. 2009). Therefore, the gap increases and disadvantaged groups become more deprived of using cultural resources. Economically, socially and culturally they are even more deprived in parallel to increased use of digital media in every part of the life and in heritage and museum context.

The rapid increase of digital media over the last couple of decades also means that they have become an important aspect of social inequalities in the context of economic development (Robinson et al. 2015; Beaunoyer et al. 2020). The main reason for this is that digital media tools are the main communication tools in the twenty-first century, from work to education to daily life (Baum et al. 2014). Therefore, they are part of the core of social, economic and political progress and development. However, they can be used to bind communities together for their sustainability and it would allow them to create their own heritage narratives, which differ from those of the state. For instance, in Australia, a digital archive, based on objects and images, was developed in collaboration with Pitjantjatjara community members who live in different locations, away from each other (Christen 2006); or in Canada with the partnership of First Nations groups and the Museum of Anthropology online resources and network created for First Nation groups to access museum collections (Rowley et al. 2010). Another good example to demonstrate these types of partnership digital projects that consider community needs and priorities is 'the Mobile Museum' project in New Ireland, Papua New Guinea to develop accessible 3D objects with the Nalik people for their material culture (Were 2014). These projects not only aim at developing digital tools, but along with collaboration with community members, the projects enable them to gain skills as well as to create access to these digital media tools. If a group does not have the skills and/or finances to use these media tools, it means they are automatically excluded and deprived of, more or less, all parts of social, cultural and economic life (see Beaunoyer et al. 2020).

This type of intense exclusion can be seen across the world and digital inequalities even exist in developed countries. For example, a recent survey that was conducted by Pew Internet and American Life Report found that 14 per cent of the American population still doesn't use the internet (Robinson et al. 2015). Similar results can also be seen in many European countries as well. Digital inequalities are even larger in underdeveloped countries, particularly in the Global South where inequalities and injustices can be seen more sharply in terms of the socio-economic context. While digital media continue to develop, they also contribute to the existing inequalities, particularly when combined with race, class and gender equality issues (Robinson et al. 2015) or, in other words, with disadvantaged groups.

Heritage sites and museums are already mainly accessed by groups with high levels of existing cultural capital and therefore, these groups are able to use these resources and are able to increase their cultural capital through using digital media tools. Conversely, disadvantaged groups, especially economically deprived groups, become more disadvantaged with the increased use of digital media because their access is limited (see Rossman and Peterson 2015) and many economically disadvantaged groups don't have the skills to use digital tools. This is linked to Bourdieu's (1986, 2005) 'capital' theory (as discussed previously). This inequality issue is obvious in the use of heritage and museums as cultural resources, as in the case of informal science learning study in London (see Dawson 2014, 2019). It is important to point out that digital media is important for diversifying audiences and reaching wider audiences (see Drotner et al. 2019). However, creating online resources also increases inequalities (Mihelj et al. 2019; Beaunoyer et al. 2020). As heritage and museum educators and specialists, we often assume and think of the positive side of digital media, which has changed the way we collect and display artefacts, and we often think that through digital media, larger and more diverse audiences can have the opportunity, for example, for content creation and curation of digitised material culture, however, these also require solid digital skills (Robinson et al. 2015). Additionally, there is limited access to these resources everywhere because of inequality that has been in place for centuries. The issue of digital inequalities, which is linked to wider socio-economic, cultural and political contexts world-wide has been neglected in heritage and museum studies. However, museums and heritage sites, as micro-organisations and spaces within larger social, cultural and political lives, have the potential to provide platforms to decrease these inequalities, through engaging communities, especially disadvantaged groups and offering digital access and skills development to use the heritage and museum cultural resources.

3 Critical Dialogues

Heritage sites and museums are spaces where materials of different cultures are presented and represented, therefore, from the perspective of cultural politics, they are very crucial public spaces (Borg and Mayo 2010) for people who can reengage and learn about either their own or other cultural dynamics and heritage. They are also significant places to develop new skills for social, cultural and economic development. Although, as discussed above, very useful theories of learning (experiential, contextual) have been developed and applied in heritage and museum contexts in praxis, critical education theories, especially critical dialogue and pedagogy, need further exploration and analysis and need to be contextualised in heritage and museum spaces. Particularly in museums in the United Kingdom and the USA, critical pedagogy in museum practice is an emerging approach as some museums and scholars have engaged with it (see Witcomb 2013), however many heritage sites and museums continue with the colonial habits of only collecting and exhibiting, rather than critically engaging with the material culture (Lynch 2016). The colonial habits of managing museums and the approach to interpreting material culture in Europe and the USA were similar to Turkey, where the public is told how to behave and what to think. In these countries that have colonial habits, museums were about legitimising colonialism (see Bennett 1995), and were designed to civilise both the home and imperial population and educate them how to live and become good consumers. This was also linked to drawing social hierarchy and maintaining inequality through a show of 'ordering and organisations' as Bennett (1995) argues, based on Michel Focuault's self-regulation and self-censorship theory.

I argue that developing critical dialogues leading to critical pedagogy (see Freire 1970) for museums and heritage sites has a great potential to tackle injustices and inequalities and design and deliver towards social justice practice. This is also crucial for equal and diverse representation and redistribution of knowledge obtained from the material culture in their practices. Museums and heritage sites should be considered as spaces where knowledge is not only to be learned but also produced, a place where legitimate knowledge can be deconstructed and reconstructed through people, a place where people come together and use it for overcoming injustices and inequalities. Having pointed out this, the museums are also a place where objects are preserved. From the point of critical pedagogy, they can also play an important role in terms of redistributing the knowledge that they contain as well as helping communities to conserve their collective memory and identity. Therefore, it is necessary for heritage and museum practices and studies to delve into critical pedagogy and determine how it can be applied effectively in cultural settings, working together with communities towards social justice.

Critical pedagogy, in both theory and practice, has been researched widely (Apple 2004; Apple et al. 2009). It developed from critical theories that were commonly applied in social sciences and humanities, bounded to pedagogical theory and politics (see Apple 2004; Apple et al. 2009). The main aim behind critical pedagogy is to respond and deal with global issues, especially socio-political, cultural and economic problems, to transform society in a progressive way. However, in most countries, like Turkey, the ideological use of education is more common in order to create 'legitimate knowledge' while conserving the state's ideology (Apple 2004). In many European museums, education was used for a long time as part of the colonial approach to dictate the legitimacy of colonialism (see Bennett 1995). Similarly, in the heritage and museum contexts, material culture was used to create 'legitimate knowledge' as in the case of the 'authorised heritage discourses' of nations who aim to promote a certain heritage that's in line with the nation state's ideology (Smith 2006; Apaydin 2018). Smith (2006, 4, 11) who introduced the idea of the 'authorised heritage discourse', describes it as:

> ... to naturalise a range of assumptions about the nature and meaning of heritage ... it promotes certain set of Western elite cultural values as being universally applicable .... It is also a professional discourse that privileges expert values and knowledge about the past and its material manifestations, and dominates and regulates professional heritage practices.

Although the use of heritage in this way can be attached to undemocratic nations in today's world, it was common in the nineteenth and twentieth centuries as I discussed in Section 2. What's also crucial is that critical education theories highlight significant questions that I believe, as heritage and museum specialists and academics, we also need to ask before designing and delivering curatorial practices and education programmes. These questions, as Apple and colleagues (2009, 3) emphasise, also set out critical design and delivery: 'What's education for?', 'How should it be carried out?', 'What should educators teach?' and 'Who should be empowered to engage in it?' These questions are also linked to the concept of democracy, as democracy is also about informing citizens for the public good and that schools in the formal education context have an important role in delivering knowledge to their citizens (Dewey 1954).

Unfortunately, in many countries, education is used to dictate certain knowledge to conserve and promote ideologies (Apple 2004). In the case of many museums around the world, for example, minority groups' heritage is neglected and museums have a strong exclusive and nationalist approach, from displays to education programmes, as in the case of Turkey (see Tureli 2014; Girard 2015; Apaydin 2018), and many more for 'imagined communities' (Anderson 2006), based on a single ethnicity to promote nationalism. In contrast to this top-down approach and ideological design and delivery, critical education is a concept that can counter these hegemonic uses of education, in other words, it is 'counter-hegemonic' as Gramsci (1971) emphasises, and it has the potential to overcome unequal and unethical creation and redistribution of knowledge in heritage sites and museums.

Whilst critical design of curatorial practices and education content and programmes are important in reflecting socio-political, cultural and economic issues, in practice it also promotes equal redistribution of knowledge, and recognition and representation of diversities as part of the social justice concept (see Fraser 2003) which sits in the centre of critical pedagogy. McLaren (1997, 13) emphasises the importance of critical pedagogy from the perspective of developing social justice education by pointing out that it aims to "reengage a social world that operates under the assumption of its collective autonomy and so remains resistant to human intervention". In the heritage and museum contexts, this refers to power relations or decentralising the power created by the top-down approach.

Therefore, the questions for heritage and museum practitioners and educators should shift towards criticality rather than only transferring 'legitimate' knowledge to audiences through displays and educational programmes. The critical questions should be reconceptualised in heritage places and museums, creating cultural settings where audiences critically engage with cultural politics and reengage with diverse cultural pasts to establish justice through a 'dialogue' with material culture. The role of educators and heritage and museum specialists is to provide the groundwork for this important aspect by keeping in mind these questions: 'Who is heritage and museum education for?', 'How should heritage site and museum curatorial practices and education programmes be designed and delivered to reflect on inequalities and injustices?', 'What should the content be of these exhibitions and programmes, and who should decide for this?', 'How can heritage site and museum practices equally redistribute knowledge?' and 'How can they act as social and cultural agents that empower individuals, groups and communities, regardless of their backgrounds, to develop organisational skills and knowledge to create equal and sustainable societies?' Although I will be reflecting on these questions with case studies in the next section, it is necessary to discuss these questions first through the reflections of John Dewey and Paulo Freire.

3.1 Critical Approaches

The first principles of social justice were established in the early twentieth century with the reflection on the concept of democracy and its interrelation with formal education. John Dewey was a philosopher who clearly and critically reflected on learning in schools and informal education. His book, *Democracy and Education* (1954), especially approached the issues that arose through injustices and inequalities within society. His approaches to democracy and education were from the same perspective because he argued that the main role of both was to inform citizens, and every individual and group should have the right to equal access to information distributed through democratic systems and education. His main focus and argument, which is still very relevant in today's formal and informal education systems in many countries around the world, was based on equal participation in education, which he argued is undermined in the state-controlled education system. He points out in his book *Democracy and Education* (1954, 58):

> ... the control is social, but individuals are part of a community, not outside of it ... the teacher exercises as a representative or agent of the interests of the group as a whole.

For Dewey, democratic education was collective and for groups as a whole (referring to everyone in society) and everyone should have the opportunity of equal access to learning. This is not only a big issue in many parts of the world in formal education, but also remains a problematic matter in informal learning settings, such as heritage sites and museums. For a large percentage of the population in many countries, museums are exclusive rather than encouraging and welcoming, and strong barriers have been developed especially for disadvantaged groups in society (Basu 2021, 53). This is linked to the idea of the institution. It is this issue that underpins calls to make museums more welcoming and needs to undergo transformation to become more inclusive (see Ahmed 2012), become a 'space' where knowledge can be produced (Lefebvre 1991) and enable access for everyone. Dewey's main reflection was on classroom-based education but he considered the classroom as a 'space' where one can discover new knowledge. Although Dewey's reflections mainly focused on formal education in the classroom and more on equal access issues rather than the content and how the content of learning should be developed, his approach to education and arguments on equal access to knowledge also sets out redistribution and access principles of social justice in today's world.

Dewey's ideas and arguments also set out why 'critical dialogue' is necessary in any learning space to construct knowledge and develop skills to take equal part in cultural, social and economic life. Paulo Freire, a critical educator and philosopher who described the unequal education system as a 'banking education model' (Freire 1970), argued that the education system doesn't reflect on dialogue but rather, it aims to transfer knowledge from teachers to students, who have no platform to question or critically think about the knowledge that's given in learning spaces. For Freire, the role of the teacher is crucial – not to transfer knowledge but to be a facilitator in learning spaces in order to establish a 'dialogue' with students (Freire and Macedo 1995). He points out that dialogue "characterises an epistemological relationship" between the facilitator and students rather than assigning them a particular task, and that dialogue is "an indispensable component of the process of both learning and knowing" (Freire and Macedo 1995, 379). Therefore, the role of teacher should be engaging with students with critical readings and objects of knowledge (Freire and Macedo 1995). Freire goes further and points out why 'dialogue' is necessary in learning spaces in his well-known book, *Pedagogy of the Oppressed* (1970, 89), and I argue that it should be a fundamental principle in heritage and museum education and engagement:

> ... dialogue is an encounter among women and men who name the world, it must not be a situation where some name on behalf of others. It is an act of creation; it must not serve as a crafty instrument for the domination of one person by another.

In the heritage and museum context, 'dialogue' does not only occur between participants and museum and heritage practitioners but also it can act to renegotiate power relations and potentially decentralises the power of heritage and museum experts to give it back to the people. For instance, through dialogue that I consider as an epistemological approach could change the nature of practice in the decision-making process in museums or heritage sites – individuals and groups have the opportunity to reengage with material culture and reinterpret it as we saw, for example, with the British Museum's 'object journeys' in the previous section. Therefore, dialogue creates an equal platform for people whose cultural identity is displayed at the museums through material culture. Or, in the case of designing exhibitions and content for education programmes, a dialogue enables participants to create knowledge by engaging with the objects and displays rather than only receiving the knowledge. This adopts a constructivist learning approach, which is based on the idea that learning is a process and participants have the opportunity to develop their own meaning and understanding through the object, in this case, the material culture (see Hooper-Greenhill 2007). As Freire emphasises, dialogue is not a 'crafty instrument' that lets dominant groups take control but rather (potentially) it eliminates oppression and gives a voice to others. This is particularly important in those authoritarian countries, such as Turkey's state museums, where minorities and disadvantaged groups are silenced and have no platform to control or to participate in learning spaces and, therefore, they are not able to take equal part in social and cultural life. This kind of oppression or, in other words, negativity towards certain groups also brings positivity for communities. In some cases, communities are able to mobilise themselves through grassroots movements as in the case of Gezi Park protests where people resisted against a top-down decision-making process to demolish Gezi Park, to reconstruct a place and therefore change the meaning of the place by imposing new meanings in parallel to the current Turkish government's, the JDP's ideology (see Apaydin 2020b). From the perspective of dialogue, Gezi Park also opened up new opportunities for those groups to develop shared values and overcome oppression by taking direct initiative against authoritarianism.

Perhaps one of the most important aspects of dialogue is that it creates a constructive learning platform where participants can engage with the object or material culture critically as part of the knowledge and learning process in the museum and heritage sites. However, in the process of knowing and learning, heritage and museum practitioners should act as facilitators and partners rather than gatekeepers and masters. The approach should be how the exhibition and education sessions could be more effectively facilitated between objects and participants through dialogue. In a way, the main argument of dialogue is similar to the idea of democratic education that was set by Dewey in the early twentieth century. This is because dialogue creates a platform for participants to engage with the knowledge equally as a whole group rather than it being dominated by one group. For Dewey, the main role of education is to inform people, as in the case of democracy. However, for Freire, education is not only informing but also creating 'critical consciousness' (see Freire 1970) to overcome the inequality issues created through oppression, as I discussed in the previous sections (Young's 'five faces of oppression').

While critical dialogue sets out a roadmap for equal participation and decentralises the power of dominant groups in museums and heritage spaces, the questions of who decides on the content and what should be taught in learning spaces are other significant parts of formal and informal learning. Considering heritage sites and particularly museums in this context, especially large museums that have collections from all over the world from historical to modern periods, who decides what should be displayed and what should be included in the content of education programmes? Or in other words, how can museum practices and curricula be developed in relation to equality and justice?

3.2 Critical Literacies

As an educator, Paulo Freire's work not only focused on effective and unoppressive learning in the classroom but his research and education models also sought to develop perhaps the most people-centred approach to develop the curriculum content for classroom facilitation. His people-centred approach or, his term of 'thematic investigation theory', also provides the groundwork for researchers to see how and what to bring into learning spaces. His main argument for this theory was that researchers or educators should focus on the ways that people are thinking within their own community context or, in other words, that the researcher or educator should consider people and communities' needs and priorities as well as the inequalities that they face to make them conscious about changing the injustice that they live with. For Freire, everyone has valuable knowledge that can contribute to this because they are part of the community as individuals, therefore, they are also part of the knowledge production that is socially constructed (Freire 1970). This theory was later developed as part of the social justice approach and applied as 'participatory action research'. However, the most important part of Freire's approach can help to develop people-centred approaches to critical literacies in learning places, especially in heritage sites and museums because his focus is to consider people's needs, priorities and the inequalities that they face. This approach also helps to support generating people-centred 'themes' in learning spaces. As it is a part of developing critical pedagogues, Freire (1970) calls this way of gathering information 'codification' that allows people to identify aspects that are related to their lives and critically reflect on them.

Viewing heritage sites and museums with their diverse collections on display and their learning resources, we can see that they have a great potential to generate themes and allow people to reflect on issues, such as trauma, displacement, loss of cultural identity and memory or climate change by enabling people to reflect on these issues based on their own experiences. This approach of bringing in critical literacies through collections, based on Freire's 'thematic investigation' theory and 'codification' method, has widely been neglected in museums and heritage sites worldwide, however, the case of the Horniman Museum[27] is a good example to contextualise this people-centred approach and to bring critical literacies into content development for education programmes and displays.

With its anthropological and natural history collections and archives, the Horniman Museum reflects not only on diversities and the issue of representation, but also aims to critically reflect and challenge socio-political and environmental

---

[27] See www.horniman.ac.uk/explore-the-collections/.

issues by bringing people's voices into collections. For instance, the Horniman Museum has thousands of cultural artefacts from various parts of Africa and Caribbean. Through a very strong ethnographic approach and 'community action research', they have aimed to bring people whose heritage is linked to these regions in Africa and Caribbean to critically interpret and discuss the meanings of these cultural artefacts for themselves today (Figures 11, 12, 13). The museum has listed the aim of this project to find effective ways to:

> Make it easier for community members to engage these collections, better understand these collections from multiple perspectives, value lived experience as an important source of knowledge, make informed decision about what actions need to be taken in the future care of these collection[28]

Figure 11 Information panel for Benin plaques that describes Horniman Museum's approach of reinterpretation of objects

---

[28] See www.horniman.ac.uk/project/community-action-research-african-and-caribbean-collec tions/.

Figure 12 Benin plaques from Benin city, Nigeria at Horniman Museum

Figure 13 Display of objects from Pacific Islanders at Horniman Museum

This approach not only gives a voice to people but it also enables people to bring their lived experiences to produce knowledge in museum space and, as part of Freire's codification process, they are able to identify aspects that are related to their priorities and lives. The work of the Horniman Museum with communities is not only critical but also the museum uses the museum as a space to develop critical pedagogues in the sense of Freire's approach (or close to his approach) to critical literacies in education. For instance, 'Rethinking Relationship and Building Trust around African Collections'[29] project aimed to bring stakeholders' voices into displays by enabling them to work directly with Horniman Museum's and several other museum's collections. In the case of its natural history and living collections, the museum highlights perhaps one of the greatest issues of climate and ecology deterioration worldwide. The museum's climate manifesto[30] (Horniman Museum 2020, 1) points out:

> Our mission is that the Horniman connects us all with global cultures and the natural environment, encouraging us to shape a positive future for the world we all share. As the only museum in London in which nature and culture can be viewed together, in both indoor and outdoor spaces, and as a much-loved and trusted institution with close to a million visits each year, the Horniman has a moral and ethical imperative to act now.

The quote from the museum's climate manifesto also emphasises the potentiality of museums towards social justice and their importance to create and form a better and sustainable future by reflecting on cultural and ecological issues. Although some argue that this can depend on museums as their collections may vary (ethnographic, anthropological or folklore; see Borg and Mayo 2010), I would argue that any museum or heritage site has a similar potential to develop critical literacy through using their space to engage with their collections from the social justice perspective. This approach can easily be adopted, even in archaeological museums, to present and critically discuss alternative, equal, non-violent and non-discriminative societies and pasts in their displays and educational programmes and resources.

For instance, considering that British Museum's large collections contain many artefacts from past cultures in different parts of the world, there is a great potential to bring critical literacies into their permanent exhibitions and learning resources and education programmes, reflecting on, for instance, the role of gender in the past societies to sustainable farming; presenting cultural connections of many artefacts to critically discuss on today's migration issues or to present the common human past. Critically reflecting on material culture to develop education programmes and exhibitions at museums also fits with the 'dialogue', 'thematic investigation' and 'codification' processes of Freire's arguments, as he considered classroom as a critical thinking space rather than

[29] See www.horniman.ac.uk/project/rethinking-relationships/.
[30] See www.horniman.ac.uk/wp-content/uploads/2020/02/horniman-climate-manifesto-final-29-jan-2020.pdf.

a space to transfer knowledge. Similarly, a museum, as a space and learning environment, can serve as a critical instrument between the visitor, audience and museum educator or curator. In the past, the British Museum attempted to do this with a pilot project, '100 Histories of 100 Worlds in 1 Object',[31] which aimed to develop new methods and approaches to reflect on museum objects with a goal of addressing the museum's role and multiculturality, to show how museums can be more democratic as a space and support diverse and ethnic audiences of the museums with collaboration of, for example, artists, educators, scholars and diaspora communities (see Brusius 2020).

Critical literacy in the museum and heritage context is as important as the museum collections, regardless of their period, cultural context and connections, and it is strongly linked to representational issues as well. For instance, while the Horniman Museum follows a very strict policy to be representative with its collections from Africa to Oceania with people-centred interpretations, many museums around the world neglect the representative aspects of critical literacy, both in their collections and displays and their educational programmes. As I discussed in the previous section, critical literacy is completely neglected in Turkey's state museums, in terms of minority groups' heritage and reflecting on inequalities and injustices through material culture. Instead, the focus is only on the state's 'authorised heritage discourse', which is based on 'Turkishness' and, therefore, Turkish heritage. This approach widely undermines not only representative aspects but also the authenticity of material culture in the museums. Whether a museum is anthropological, archaeological or art based, as a space, they all have the potential of being representative to their audiences and can reflect on inequalities and injustices, particularly through critical collaborations with communities, the public and their wider audiences.

3.3 Critical Collaborations

Particularly in the last couple of decades, we have witnessed increased collaboration in museums and heritage sites with the public through participatory approaches. This approach has become the policy of many international and national organisations. For instance, UNESCO made it compulsory to include communities into the decision-making process as part of attaining World Heritage Site status, and many international organisations and museum associations declared the importance of including the public into the decision-making process and collaborating with them, as in the case of the Museum Association in the United Kingdom. Although these are progressive developments in terms of

---

[31] See https://100histories100worlds.org/project-history/.

making heritage sites and museums more multivocal by getting different voices into the decision-making process, the approach that heritage specialists and organisations take is still 'top down' because only representatives of communities and stakeholders are included in the decision-making process and the research and work are still only conducted by the 'experts'. Conversely, critical collaboration takes a strong people-centred approach to include people into decision-making by bringing every individual and group view through the concept of Paulo Freire's (1970) dialogue. This requires strong participatory action research that is also based on Freire's (1970) 'thematic investigation method'. Freire (1970) notes that any action taken that excludes any community member or groups will lead to a top-down approach and won't be valid. Freire considers collaboration as a dialogue and researchers or professionals are equal with community members as part of mutual trust. Research and, therefore, the work agenda, must emerge from the needs and priorities of the people (Freire 1970) rather than, as we often do, from the imposition of our own agendas in the heritage and museum and upon audiences.

Critical collaboration is one of the key concepts in social justice heritage practices and education because our main resource is people who develop the material culture that they ascribe meanings to, develop values of and construct their cultural identities around. Therefore, for critical collaboration, every voice matters, and to include every voice in curatorial and educational practices is the core characteristic of critical collaboration, which is also strongly linked to ethnographic methodologies. One of the great pitfalls in ethnographic studies, particularly common in anthropological and heritage studies, is that researchers or professionals usually conduct their studies as an outsider with possible biases and prejudices and they may not be able to understand every dynamic between communities and members. In contrast, in a critical collaboration, as part of the dialogical process, research and data collection are done by the community members themselves.

A case study that was conducted in the Chatham Islands, where researchers collaborated with the Moriori people to develop a cultural database and heritage management plan (see Hollowell and Nicholas 2009), is a good example to demonstrate critical collaboration. In the case of the Emotive project (see next section), for example, we trained and employed young locals to collaborate and conduct research together with us. A similar critical collaboration was done by Smith and colleagues (2019) in Australia. While researching indigenous heritage, they didn't just collaborate with Australian indigenous community members but also, most importantly, employed indigenous researchers to collaborate who led the research, took initiatives in every step of the project and published results. Whilst this is an ethical and people-centred approach that can potentially expose the dynamics, priorities and needs of the community, it also empowers and enables indigenous community members, people who have been oppressed and excluded from decision-making processes about their own heritage because of injustices, to develop skills. Thus, they can have a voice in the social, political and economic life as well as develop 'capitals' as Bourdieu (1986) argued.

Critical collaboration is not only significant from the perspective of including people into research stages, data collection, interpretation of material culture and museum displays but also it is ethical, as it brings every dynamic of the community, their needs and priorities into the light. Or, in other words, when developing museum displays or educational resources and programmes, communities should not only be considered for consultation but rather, the main approach should be 'the work cannot be done' without communities (Lynch 2014). It is still common in heritage and museum practices to consider communities and individuals as part of the deficit model (see Dawson 2019): either they don't have sufficient knowledge or they are not motivated to take part. Conversely, critical collaboration through a dialogical process deconstructs the deficit model as it considers individuals and communities as a group who are indispensable for developing critical pedagogy (Freire 1970). Therefore, in heritage and museum practice, individuals and communities should be considered the main part of the work rather than a 'support tool'.

Although current heritage and museum practices and organisations have progressively aimed to deal with this issue through various kinds of engagement strategies, the establishment of the main principles of 'critical collaboration' between heritage sites, museums and communities is still vague. Bernadette Lynch, who undertook a substantial analysis of collaboration between museums and communities, points out in her report, *Whose cake is it anyway?* (Lynch 2011, 8, 2014), the importance of this component to bring change to the museums and, most importantly, to decentralise the power of top-down approach at museums:

> ... a process of real change can only be set in motion through participation, both as the means and long-term purpose of the work. By shifting the concept of public engagement to focus on capability development through the active participation must be central to helping the organisation bring about change, with local people taking responsibility for their museum or gallery, and gaining valuable experience of active citizenship in the process.

Lynch's reflection, based on analysing twelve museums in the United Kingdom, also emphasises why 'critical collaboration' should be indispensable for museums and heritage sites. While active participation brings 'change' in how organisations function, it also decentralises the power of the organisation as part of the dialogical process that Freire (1970) emphasised. Critical collaboration also provides a platform for individuals and groups within the community to develop skills. This opportunity, in parallel to Bourdieu's concept of 'capital', has the potential to decrease inequality and give a chance to disadvantaged groups to socially, culturally and economically develop themselves and engage with heritage and museums more effectively to develop further skills. However, in many museums and heritage sites, collaboration has become more of a 'buzzword', and there is little critical collaboration and giving voice to people; it has become ineffective in practice and method (see Lynch 2016). This is, of course, something more to do with power sharing in cultural settings. Community members have often been considered as subjects for museum and heritage site practices rather than as active agents and main drivers of museum and heritage sites as spaces. Bernadette Lynch (2016, 21) describes this entanglement of participatory approach in museums as:

> ... this continuing situation is that the notion of centre/periphery/ 'us' and 'them' is still alive and well, and it continues to undermine the learning and participatory efforts of these well-meaning museums and their staff members. By placing people in the position of *beneficiaries*, the museums exercise invisible power ...

This is an embedded discourse that can be seen in many museums worldwide as part of continued ideological and colonial use of museums and heritage sites. As it was discussed in Sections 3.1 and 3.2, in his 'banking education model', Freire (1970) called the relationship between students and teacher 'object and subject', where one side transfers the knowledge and other side receives it. Students or communities in this model are considered as 'beneficiaries' as Lynch points out in the museum context. In contrast to this approach that undermines the actual voice and contribution of people in museum and heritage site practice, critical collaboration places people in the centre of any practice and work of museums and heritage sites by allowing people to make decisions reflecting their needs and priorities.

3.4 Critical Contacts

Critical dialogue is crucial in creating democratic platforms for heritage sites and museums to develop critical literacies and to engage with their audiences, local communities and the public more effectively from the bottom-up perspective and to make people the main drivers of cultural organisations. Another crucial benefit of critical dialogue is that it does not only bring heritage and museum experts into contact with communities but that it also brings culturally, ethnically, socially and economically diverse communities into contact to learn about cultural dynamics, values and meanings through material culture in the museum and heritage space. Here, my argument is based on indirect 'contact': material culture and displays present tangible and intangible heritage to different audiences. Considering museum and heritage sites as a space that brings groups and communities into contact, what benefits would it bring? Why is it important in a wider sense to deal with the injustices that the world has (prejudice, biases, racism as well as violence against certain groups, especially towards minorities)?

In his book, *The Nature of Prejudice* (1954), psychologist and theorist Gordon Allport reflects on the discourses of prejudice in a society that eventually lead to 'bias', 'discrimination', 'attack of violence' and 'annihilation' of culturally different groups. He discusses that the majority group in a society develop negative speech and stereotypes against minority groups because they are not in 'contact' with these groups that are culturally and ethnically different from the majority of a society. This further develops to excluding minority groups, then discrimination, attacks and violence occur to these disadvantaged groups. This kind of violence can be seen in many parts of the world, either systematic or individual. To prevent prejudices, racism and violence against ethnically and culturally different groups, Allport (1954) developed the 'intergroup contact theory', which has been used in social psychology and applied in many contexts today. Allport emphasised that prejudice is the same as antipathy, which is developed through negative emotions. The main idea and argument of contact theory are to combat bias developed among the majority group(s) in a society because of negative emotions, against diverse backgrounds and disadvantaged groups. Through promoting tolerance, recognition, acknowledgement and acceptance, the idea of 'contact' has a great potential to prevent prejudice, racism and violence in a society and has the potential to create a platform to negotiate historical issues between groups.

I consider heritage sites and museums as social, political and economic spaces and along with their cultural importance, there is a great potential to make 'critical contact' between different identity, ethnic and cultural groups, who learn and critically think about differences and develop empathy. However, Allport (1954) also points out that in order to reduce prejudice, 'contact' needs to happen in an equal and cooperative platform. This is perhaps one of the greatest issues in heritage context in many parts of the world. Whilst one heritage is promoted and others are undermined, consciously or unconsciously, this will increase prejudices. In the case of Turkey, for example, although the Armenian material culture of the past can be seen everywhere in the country, it is not allocated space in the museum displays or used as an educational resource, as I discussed in the previous section. In many museums in Europe and USA, indigenous people's material culture or objects from the Global South is displayed from a very top-down perspective. However, my main argument for critical contact in museums and heritage sites is not only about learning about other cultures through material culture to reduce or totally overcome prejudice, but also through enabling community members to use these spaces to renegotiate the past and historical issues and to reflect on contemporary problems. Anthropologist James Clifford (1997) calls this space 'the contact zone' to encounter challenges (also see Dibley 2005; Boast 2011). He points out (1997, 192, 193):

> ... when museums are seen as contact zones, their organising structure as a collection becomes an ongoing historical, political, moral relationship – a power charged set of exchanges, of push and pull.

While this is strongly linked to the 'dialogical process' discussed in the previous section through the democratic approach, critical literacies and collaboration, this is more to do with the management of museums and heritage sites and the question of to what extent they are open to using their space as a contact zone for communities and how displays and educational programmes and resources as tools can support this critical contact zone. Clifford (1997) exemplifies this decentralising power and recreating museum space as a contact zone with the case study of Portland Art Museum where indigenous material culture is displayed. He observed that while the Portland Art Museum staff were very eager to discuss their displays on indigenous material culture with indigenous people's representatives, indigenous people were keen to reengage with the past, historical facts as well as contemporary issues that they were having. In other words, there were great differences between the agendas of the museum staff and the community, an issue that is common across the world.

The agendas of museum staff undermine what the community wants, and they neglect and ignore the relationship and links of past events to the present as well as their role in establishing the future. For instance, the traumas that American indigenous people faced in the past still affect them widely in the present because it is a continuous process until it is acknowledged and recognised (Estes 2019). In a way, the attitude of the Portland Art Museum also demonstrates a strong top-down approach in which experts aim to impose knowledge through certain agendas against developing critical literacies in the museum by excluding the needs, priorities and views of indigenous people. However, following this controversy and tension between indigenous community and the museum, what Clifford observes is that the Portland Art Museum becomes a space where issues were discussed and renegotiated. Most importantly, they come into 'contact' and dialogues were developed in this 'zone' where different cultures can also come into contact and negative emotions ('antipathy') can be turned into empathy and, therefore, help to reduce prejudice and prevent all forms of racism and violence against certain groups.

In a way, Clifford's observation at the Portland Art Museum demonstrates the dilemmas that many museums in Europe and the USA have when displaying cultural objects. While in theory many museums attempt to shift their approach towards a more people-centred approach rather than an object based, many museums still follow the traditional, twentieth century way of managing museums and heritage sites. They may have taken on calls for community participation, but this is often tokenistic rather than truly collaborative. Cultures and the material culture and objects where meanings, values and memories are embedded, is certainly important, however, what's more import-ant is the people who develop that culture and material culture. Using museums and heritage sites as a critical contact zone is not only important to bring people into contact and prevent conflicts, prejudice, biases and all forms of racism (Allport 1954), but it is also significant from the perspectives of recognition and representation of communities in the public space, as well as redistributing knowledge that's obtained through the material culture in the museum.

4 Social Justice Heritage Practice

Section 2 dealt with authoritarian, global and critical practices and Section 3 focused on ways to critically engage and to use museums and heritage settings through the development of a 'dialogue', thereby overcoming oppressive forces in the heritage and museum context. In this section, I will discuss 'social justice' through the 'redistribution', 'recognition' and 'representation' concepts while contextualising them in heritage and museum settings with case studies. I will also develop a framework for social justice heritage practices. The redistribution, recognition and representation dimensions of social justice, developed by critical theorist Nancy Fraser (1998, 2003, 2013), are very important in decreasing inequalities in the heritage and museum context. Although these three concepts have been applied well in social, educational and political sciences, the same cannot be said about the museum and heritage context. Representation, recognition and redistribution are strongly linked with each other and they expose the discourses of inequalities and injustices in the wider social, political and economic context as well as in the heritage and museum framework.

4.1 Redistribution

Heritage sites and museums are resources that contribute to the social, cultural and economic capitals of individuals and groups who are then able to develop skills that can be used in any part of life. Though, in the context of heritage and museums, it is crucial to consider sharing resources equally, increasing access for all and enabling everyone to develop skills. Fraser's redistributive claim is based on equal redistribution of wealth between individuals and groups in a society, in other words, equal access to the economic capital that Bourdieu (1986, 2005) discusses. However, especially with the introduction of the free-market and neoliberal policies, access to these resources has become more difficult for groups who were already economically deprived and who were not able to access economic capital in a very hierarchical society (see Harvey 2005). So, what is the position of heritage sites and museums within this hierarchical structure? What does redistribution mean in the heritage and museum context? What do heritage and museums have to do with wealth and economic distribution?

Nancy Fraser's 'redistribution' claim sits in the centre of equal distribution of economic wealth and resources. She discusses the inequalities of distribution between communities and countries – some take large portion of resources but some don't take or get anything at all. This is similar to the heritage and museum context because these resources are mostly used by people who have the most economic, social and cultural capital, while disadvantaged groups are deprived from using and obtaining equal distribution of these resources. Fraser (2003, 7) points out:

> ... redistributive claims, which seek a more just distribution of resources and wealth. Examples include claims for redistribution from the North to the South, from the rich to the poor, and (not so long ago) from the owners to the workers. To be sure, the recent resurgence of free-market thinking has put proponents of redistribution on the defensive.

Fraser's approach to redistribution is based on inequalities and injustices as it is similar to Bourdieu's theory of social, cultural and economic capital: the group who has the capital also controls the resources. Although, as Fraser points out, the intense neoliberal policies have accelerated and exacerbated inequalities and put 'redistributive claims' in an even more difficult position as the gap between the poor and wealthy increased, this type of injustice and inequality can be seen throughout the course of human history in different forms (Graeber and Wengrow 2021). A contemporary example in the heritage context is European museums, which emerged from colonialism and continue to hold display objects, artefacts and monuments of the Global South whose resources were consumed by imperial powers (see Bennett 1995, 2004, 2017; Joy 2020). This especially demonstrates how one group can control another's cultural resources. However, the main cause of inequality has always been accessing resources.

Throughout this Element, I emphasise that heritage sites and museums are far more than just places for displaying objects and material culture – they are the resource for developing skills that are strongly linked to cultural, economic and social capital. When an individual has economic and social capital and they also have access to cultural capital that leads to further skills development. They then are able to use these skills to increase their economic and social capital. This can clearly be seen in the visitor profiles of museums in many parts of the world, where disadvantaged groups don't or can't go to heritage sites, museums and galleries to interact with cultural capital and, therefore, are unable to develop skills. These can be knowledge or the skills to engage with material culture or displays in museums and galleries. Dawson's (2019) case study that focused on informal science learning within five minority communities in London is a good example. The results of her study show that many people from disadvantaged communities don't go to the Science Museums because they do not already possess the knowledge or technical skills to engage with objects, material culture or activities of museum.

There are many discourses on this inequality, of course, and they vary in different contexts. For instance, Kinsley (2016) links this inequality to the admission fees for US museums, which create access barriers for the public. In the case of Turkey, the admission fee is also a big barrier for economically disadvantaged groups, who are not able to afford to go to the museums and heritage sites. However, in other countries, such as the United Kingdom, many museums are free but are still mostly accessed by individuals and groups who have more economic, social and cultural capital as indicated through various reports[32] (see also Ipsos MORI 2011).

Museums and heritage sites are spaces where knowledge of past and present cultures is stored, presented and used for different purposes and used to produce new knowledge, as discussed in Section 2. However, engaging, accessing and benefiting from these knowledge resources, from the point of equal redistribution, also requires strong skills that individuals and groups need to have. This shifts the focus towards what museums and heritage sites can do to enable disadvantaged groups to engage with cultural resources and cultural spaces so they can benefit from the redistribution of knowledge that is embedded in the material culture and heritage. This is, of course, related to strong and innovative community engagement, partnership and collaboration strategies that have become common museums that aim to bring diverse voices into museums. However, most disadvantaged groups avoid visiting or using cultural settings because of skills requirements for using these cultural resources and spaces (see Dawson 2019). So, it is not the question of what museums and heritage sites can do to bring more visitors from diverse backgrounds to the museums but rather, it

---

[32] See www.artscouncil.org.uk/sites/default/files/download-file/East_England_2016_17_0.pdf.

should be how museums can take these resources to the communities to enable them to develop skills through using these resources.

For the redistribution of knowledge that is stored at the museums through material culture and heritage, bringing disadvantaged communities into a museum and including them into interpretation and display stages is one way of doing this. However, I argue that the work of museums and heritage sites shouldn't be limited to the four walls of the museum, and the focus should shift towards engaging communities outside of the walls. One way of doing this is to take the knowledge of material culture to the communities through developing strong community collaborations, partnerships and offering training for skills development for all community members, regardless of age, instead of expecting communities to visit museums and heritage sites.

The work of Hackney Museum, which I will discuss and contextualise in relation to social justice concept in the next section, is a good example to demonstrate how a museum can carry their work outside of museum walls, engage with all community groups in the vicinity and develop partnerships with community organisations. Similar, but from a different perspective, is the work and aims of the Museum of Homelessness,[33] which is a community-driven museum run by people who have experienced homelessness. Including those who had these experiences into the museum work not only helps to reduce inequality and increase equal distribution of knowledge but it also gives those people the opportunity to develop skills through museum projects and as such, this skills development could impact social and economic capital.

Fraser (2003) points out the second dimension of social justice claim, recognition, should not be considered separately from the redistribution dimension because they are both linked to the economy and politics. Therefore, in the heritage and museum context, engaging communities outside of the museum walls and sites to redistribute the knowledge and provide tools for skills development also requires strong recognition.

4.2 Recognition

Fraser (2003, 7) outlines 'recognition' as:

> ... Today, however, we increasingly encounter a second type of social-justice claim in the 'politics of recognition'. Here the goal, in its most plausible form, is a difference-friendly world, where assimilation to majority or dominant cultural norms is no longer the price of equal respect. Examples include claims for the recognition of the distinctive perspectives of ethnic, 'racial', and sexual minorities, as well as of gender difference.

---

[33] See https://museumofhomelessness.org/.

The second claim of social justice is 'recognition' that seeks to acknowledge differences in the world in terms of racial, sexual, gender and ethnic differentiation. This claim is basically centred round diversities that is the range of differences among people from race to ethnicity, sexual orientation to gender identity, class, age, religious or political beliefs, physical ability and many more. Recognition is an important issue in the heritage and museum context because most nation states have used material culture to prove their ownership rights or to create their 'imagined community' (Anderson 2006) based on a single ethnicity and race by misrecognising diversities. Although the two claims (redistribution and recognition) seem to reflect different inequalities, they both need to be considered together because they are strongly connected to each other both in the heritage and museum and in the wider socio-political contexts. Fraser (2003) points out that social justice needs to be both 'redistribution' and 'recognition'. Redistribution may be considered as class politics and recognition as identity politics (Fraser 2003) but unequal distribution and misrecognition fuel each other in the sense of economic, social and cultural life of today's world. As unequal distribution increased with the free-market policies across the world, this has also motivated undemocratic countries to become authoritarian (see Brown 2019) and to use the resources of minorities who are also not being recognised by the states. In other words, in many countries such as Turkey, neoliberalism also motivated and fuelled authoritarian regimes that used minority groups' resources for the benefit of the majority. Because of unequal redistribution, the misrecognition of diversities and the undermining of the idea and the reality of a multicultural society, disadvantaged groups, such as those with racial and sexual differences, are not able to find social, cultural, political and economic platforms to represent themselves and to be represented. However, this oppressive and unequal approach has often resulted with emergence of grassroots movements in Turkey, as in the case of the Gezi Park movement or heritage and community organisations and NGOs such as *Anadolu Kültür* mentioned earlier, to promote and represent under-voiced groups in social and cultural life.

Fraser (2013) points out that the misrecognition of gender, identity, ethnicity or, in other words, a denial of the diversity of all societies also strongly contributes to the inequality and injustices in a society. Misrecognition happens very often in our society, it is something that all disadvantaged groups face, perhaps on a daily basis. Misrecognition is very much linked to holding social, economic and cultural capital as groups who hold these capitals also are the dominant group who often undermine, ignore or exclude members of the disadvantaged groups who are not able to participate in the economic, social and cultural life. As Fraser (1997, 14) emphasises, one culture dominates another and misplaces the cultural values of those disadvantaged groups. She further states:

> ... cultural domination (being subjected to patterns of interpretation and communication that are associated with another culture and are alien and/or hostile to one's own); nonrecognition (being rendered invisible by means of the authoritative representational, communicative, and interpretative practices of one's culture); and disrespect (being routinely maligned or disparaged in stereotypic public cultural representations and/or in everyday life interactions).

This, of course, does not only happen in daily life – it gets more structural at the institutional level, as I discussed in Section 2 about how minority groups and their heritage are not recognised at the state level, including in education and cultural settings, in the case of museums and heritage sites in Turkey. Misrecognition or nonrecognition not only further marginalises those groups, whose identities are not acknowledged and recognised, but it also increases inequalities because excluding them from cultural resources also means excluding them from skills development that contributes to their social and economic lives. Similar examples can be found in other parts of the world, such as the misrecognition of African American identities and heritage at some of US museums and minority group heritage and history at European museums (see Coffee 2008). Additionally, many museums across the world still neglect sexual/gender differences and their associated history and heritage.

In the heritage and museum sector and in wider socio-political contexts, recognition not only means acknowledging the existence of a particular group, but it is also about giving status to those groups so that they can equally take part in the social, economic and cultural life. This is also directly linked to the redistributive claim of social justice. In the heritage and museum context, recognition falls into two categories. First, museums that store the material culture of the past and present cultures can be more diverse and inclusive in how they display and curate their objects related to their diverse audiences. This doesn't just impact only on the recognition of minorities but it also has the potential to motivate disadvantaged groups to engage with museums and heritage sites more effectively. Hood's (2004) study on African-American visitors shows that they feel unmotivated to engage in museums because of the misrecognition of their identity, history and heritage. Second, collecting and developing collections is often museums' main priority (see Macdonald 2006), however, these important aspects are widely driven by material and object-based approaches that undermine current socio-political issues as well as diversities of the society. The material culture of the past is a significant aspect, of course, as meanings are ascribed, values are developed and identities are constructed by individuals, groups and communities (Ashworth et al. 2007). However, I consider museums as a space and critical contact zone that should be able to reflect on contemporary diversities of society through collecting the contemporary material culture of the communities, who can also collaborate and contribute to the recognition of their identities. This is also strongly linked to the representation dimension of social justice.

4.3 Representation

In her work, *Scales of Justice* (2009), Nancy Fraser further develops the main cores of the 'redistribution' and 'recognition' concepts of social justice with the 'representation' dimension. She points out the importance of 'representation' by emphasising why it is necessary towards a social justice in the current world of inequality and injustice (2009, 17):

> ... the political dimension of justice is concerned chiefly with representation. At one level, which pertains to the boundary-setting aspect of the political, representation is a matter of social belonging. What is at issue here is inclusion in, or exclusion from, the community of those entitled to make justice claims on one another. At another level, which pertains to the decision-rule aspect, representation, concern the procedures that structure public processes of contestation. Here, what is at issue are the terms on which those included in the political community air their claims and adjudicate their dispute.

Representation of justice is linked to the political dimension in participatory or collaborative democracy. In other words, she links justice to the bottom-up decision-making process and people-centred approach, where people have a voice in the political process, including its contexts and structure, which also have the potential for enabling recognition and redistribution (2009). She explores 'representation' and builds on it by adding three different sub-dimensions: 'ordinary-political, framings, and metapolitical'. Ordinary-political representation concerns the process of decision-making and focuses on the important terms that are also significant in the heritage and museum context, such as 'inclusion', and questions how diverse voices are included in this process.

The framings dimension focuses again on the process but looks at the structure of this collaborative decision-making process (Calvert and Warren 2014) by questioning who is recognised and allowed into this decision-making process. The third dimension of representation, 'metapolitical', is about where and how participation takes place. In other words, how the power of decision-making shifts from the state level to institutions. For instance, UNESCO is a global governance institution that, combined with nation states, has the power to make decisions about cultural heritage sites, although the decisions are still made by state parties (see Meskell 2018).

The representation concept of social justice can be divided into three categories in the heritage and museum context: (1) the inclusion of diverse voices or, in other words, bringing the diverse voices of the community into the decision-making process in heritage and museum work; (2) how this process can be more collaborative without excluding any individual or groups in heritage and museum work and (3), if decisions are made on an institutional level, as in the case of UNESCO, or on the community level; in other words, are experts or museum and heritage specialists imposing their agenda on communities during this process?

The discourses of inclusion and exclusion in the heritage and museum context, especially in terms of reflecting diverse audiences, have long been debated and researched, as I discussed above (recognition section; also see Sandell 2003; Coffee 2008) and many museums and heritage sites have innovatively reflected on this issue. However, the representation dimension from the perspective of including diverse voices in the decision-making process is still lacking in heritage sites and museums because it is about sharing power and this often conflicts with the organisational structure of institutions. Fraser's sharing of power or decentralising the institution's power is also about 'parity of participation' that aims to lead to justice through ensuring that all members of society participate as peers in social, cultural and political life (2009, 18). In recent years, many heritage sites and museums have taken a participatory approach that aimed to include people into the decision-making process for their work and projects, which have had positive impacts (see Lynch 2011). This is especially the case with small museums, which have established effective relationships with their local audiences (see below for Hackney Museum; Lynch and Alberti 2010; Lynch 2011; Museum of the Home[34] and Sutton House[35] and many more, especially in the United Kingdom), who have contributed to the design and decision-making process of projects (see Lynch 2011). However, how 'parity' works in those participatory projects is still fluid. Collaborating with stakeholders, such as community members and audiences, has the potential to create 'parity' in heritage and museum work and could have a more positive outcome than those projects that are designed only using the expert knowledge of curators, museum educators and specialists.

For most museum or heritage site management plans, the participatory approach is defined as either consulting the stakeholders and communities for museum projects (see Lynch and Alberti 2010). However, because parity of participation aims to reach the goal of social justice through enabling

---

[34] See www.museumofthehome.org.uk/.

[35] See www.nationaltrust.org.uk/sutton-house-and-breakers-yard/primary-learning.

redistribution and recognition, the idea of the participatory approach in the heritage and museum context needs to shift towards a 'critical collaboration', whereby museum and heritage projects become community-run projects, as in the case of Museum of Homelessness (Turtle and Turtle 2020). Additionally, even in a participatory democracy, not everyone is able to attend the political decision-making process because some groups may be more dominant than others (see Fraser 2009). This reflects in a different way in the heritage and museum settings, as Dawson (2019) demonstrates in the case of the Informal Science Learning project. Dawson found that groups who are not skilled (in terms of education) are not able to even engage with science learning in informal educational settings, therefore, those groups of communities will not even be motivated to take part in decision-making process. Therefore, in order to enable 'parity' in participation, museums need to offer skills development programmes so that different and diverse parts of the community can contribute to the heritage and museum activities. In the sections below, I will discuss Hackney Museum in relation to the redistribution, recognition and representation concepts – the work and projects of Hackney Museum over the years are important examples of how social justice practice and education programmes at museums can be developed. Then I will discuss the Emotive storytelling project to demonstrate how education programmes at heritage sites can critically engage with their audiences, and collaborate and develop skills through digital media tools and in-person experiences.

4.4 People-Centred Heritage

Throughout this Element, I have emphasised the importance of the social, political and economic roles of heritage and museums. I stressed that heritage sites and museums, as spaces, have the potential to decrease inequalities and injustices faced by a large proportion of the world's population through the use of the material culture, collections, displays and the museums and heritage sites themselves, as a space. In other words, I consider the main role of museums and heritage is to create a platform for the equal redistribution of knowledge, to provide skills for the development of individuals and communities, to recognise and promote diversities in order to decrease prejudice and any forms of racism and bias, and to be representative of the whole community through strong sustainable partnerships.

Hackney Museum,[36] in northeast London, is a small community museum, funded by the local authority, that demonstrates how a museum can develop social justice practice that confronts inequalities and injustices. One of the most

---

[36] See https://hackney-museum.hackney.gov.uk/.

important characteristics of Hackney Museum, and the main reason why I use it as a case study here, is that the museum focuses on one of the greatest social and political issues of the past and present and makes it the main focus of its displays: migration. The topic of 'migration' has been engaged and studied intensively by academics in heritage and museum studies to reflect on memory, politics and identity (see Gouriévidis 2014). In the case of Hackney Museum, communities themselves are involved in developing exhibitions through donating and interpreting material culture or objects that they have valued and represent their identities. At Hackney Museum, this focus on migration stretches from the Anglo-Saxon period to recent times of the Hackney neighbourhood, and this migration theme is reflected in their collections, displays, education programmes and learning resources, as well as the contemporary collecting strategies of the museum.

4.4.1 People's Platform

The Hackney Borough of London is a very multicultural district that is home to many people from Africa to Asia and other parts of the world. In addition, recent archaeological research indicates that migration to the Hackney area dates back to the Anglo-Saxon period and continues today. With its collecting and display strategy, Hackney Museum reflects this diverse history of the past and present well. It displays the material cultures of its community members, who donated material culture such as suitcases, music instruments and photo collections that represent both the individual and the collective memories and the collective identities of each community in the Hackney district (see Figures 14 and 15). Displaying material cultures that are also embedded with memories, identities and a collective cultural identity of those diverse communities leads to a strong recognition dimension of social justice, as discussed by Fraser (2003).

As mentioned above, the recognition and redistribution dimensions are strongly linked to each other and should be considered together. For instance, in the case of Hackney Museum's collecting and displaying strategy, it is not only significant for recognising the diverse and multicultural structure and community cohesion of the district but also this diverse approach leads to 'direct contact': that is, different cultures are introduced to other community groups that are culturally distinct but able to learn about one another from the displays and collections. The project, 'Hello Cazenove', in 2014 is a good example to demonstrate this and shows how museums can reach out and create a platform for their communities outside of the museum's walls.

This project combined a range of activities and events with the communities of Cazenove Road – a street in Hackney – who represent many different ethnic,

Figure 14 Immigration display at Hackney Museum

religious and economic backgrounds, and created an exhibition at the museum where all community members contributed. The exhibition 'Side by Side: Living in Cazenove' was combined of many creative works including artwork, installations as well as films that were produced by residents of Cazenove, local schools and supported by professionals such as filmmakers and artists. This project not only provided for diverse communities to have a voice in displaying their own culture but also, as a platform, it brought diverse groups and cultures into contact to introduce themselves one to another. Emma Wick (7 June 2021), the Hackney Museum manager, pointed out in an interview that 'it was a very productive project where different backgrounds of community members attended and contributed events and exhibition'.

This is also directly linked to Gordon Allport's (1954) 'contact' theory as the Hackney Museum is enabling different and diverse community groups to get into contact through creating community platforms and using material culture where meanings, values and memories of certain cultures are embedded.

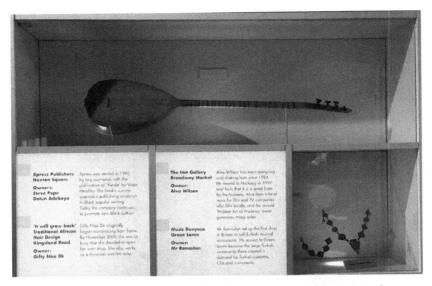

Figure 15 Display of musical instruments of the Turkish community at Hackney Museum

This people-centred approach of Hackney Museum also reflects my argument to use the museum as a 'critical contact zone' where community members come together and raise and discuss issues or, in other words, develop a dialogue that can further develop platforms to negotiate social, political and economic issues. Hackney Museum (2017, 1) states:

> Our Platform space in the museum is for community exhibitions. To highlight issues, challenges and things that groups of people want to speak up or speak out about and support the research, interpretation or development of our collections. This is a space where we hand over the message to local people. From community groups, to groups wanting greater visibility for their message, to people wanting to bring to light hidden histories or reveal previously unspoken or challenging truths.

Although there are important differences between indigenous and migrant communities, this is similar to the case study of the Portland Art Museum where the museum created a space for American indigenous and local community members to discuss social and political issues, as discussed in Clifford (1997) and above (also see Boast 2011). The platform that was created by the Hackney Museum for local community members and groups is not only important for giving a voice to community members about the direction, work and exhibitions of the museum but it is also crucial because it enables them to renegotiate past issues that have traumatised many community members, such as Syrian and Ukrainian refugees who had to flee from the war in their respective countries.

It is common for many museums to consult and obtain views from community members about the exhibitions and projects that they run. However, in the context of social justice, in order to decrease inequalities and injustices, the question really should be to what extent these works relate to the community's present social, political and historical issues. In this sense, the statement of Hackney Museum is very important and is an excellent example: as they state, their platform is a place where community members reflect on any issues or challenges that they want to raise. While this is important from the perspective of the representation dimension of social justice, it is also significant in that it shows how a museum can be used from the perspective of a people-centred approach that considers the needs, priorities and voices of individuals and groups rather than imposing themes and issues through a top-down approach.

Creating a platform to give a voice to community members also enables individuals and groups to develop a dialogue in this critical contact zone, as discussed in the previous section, and it has the potential to initiate a dialogical process where counter-narratives can be discussed. Mikhail Bakhtin (1981, 84), the language philosopher and cultural historian, in his essays *The Dialogic Imagination: Four Essays*, points out the importance of subjectivities and how they can emerge through narrating time and space in his concept, 'chronotope': In the literary artistic chronotope ... time ... thickens, takes on flesh, becomes artistically visible; likewise, space becomes charged and responsive to the movements of time, plot and history.

Developing a dialogue is significant in three ways. First, it enables people to bring different views and opinions. This can include issues related to museum practices or social and economic issues that community members want to reflect on. This in turn can help museums to learn about the dynamics of the community groups and their issues so they can reflect on these issues in their displays or educational materials as part of developing critical literacies. This is an issue, especially for museums that are entangled in making decisions on, for example, what to display, what the content of learning programmes should be or how to develop these resources and exhibitions from a people-centred approach. This is similar to Freire's (1970) argument on developing content for classroom through participatory action research that focuses on people who develop and create knowledge rather than imposing knowledge that is created by teachers. Emma Winch (7 June 2021), the heritage learning manager of Hackney Museum, points out that: It is important to give voice and power to community members and community ownership at the museum is important. Because of this, we even changed the post of 'curator' to 'community officer' at the

Hackney Museum . . . museums are not about curators and their ideas and work but what comes from the communities is important.

Second, this type of platform is significant in its impact on reducing prejudices, racism and developing empathy for each other because people from different ethnic, identity and sexual orientation groups come into direct contact with each other. This platform gives people the chance to get to know about other cultures, reflecting Allport's (1954) contact theory. This kind of platform for the communities enables them to develop a sustainable society where all differences and diversities are known and acknowledged.

Third, a critical platform empowers community members to take a role in the cultural development of their community. This also has the potential to overcome the 'marginalisation' dimension of oppression (Young 1990 and discussed in Section 2). In contrast to the situation in Turkey, where the oppression consumes the cultural products of minority groups and excludes disadvantaged communities from the cultural, social and political life, a platform like this, for community members, leads to inclusion and gives the community members a chance to develop themselves culturally, and therefore economically and socially.

Throughout this section, I emphasise the importance of being able to develop skills and this is based on the 'cultural capital' theory of Bourdieu (1986) who argues that people who have good access to education and other cultural institutions are able to develop skills and thus can take a share from social, economic and cultural capitals. Therefore, museums and heritage sites, as public spaces, should be able to offer this opportunity, especially to those who are disadvantaged because of inequality and injustices in every part of social, economic and political life.

4.4.2 Skills Development

Offering skills development is important in the heritage and museum settings because it is directly related to inequalities. Looking through the lens of Bourdieu's 'cultural capital' theory and the unequal redistribution of resources theory of Nancy Fraser, what we can see in cultural settings is that inequalities and injustices have increased even more because digital media is the dominant means of communication in most all museums and heritage sites in today's world. This technological development, of course, has positive impacts but it also has many pitfalls and contributes to existing inequalities. Digital inequalities already exist and are clearly seen in broad range of areas, for instance, gender, race and class, as well as economics and politics (see Robinson et al. 2015), as discussed in Section 2. In other words, the increased use of digital media also increases the already existing inequalities (also see Mihelj et al. 2019). The inequalities in using museums and heritage sites are not necessarily only related to digital media but also because to use these resources already requires a certain level of knowledge and skills (see Dawson 2019).

One of the main reasons that inequalities exist and is increasing in society is that whilst some groups are able to use resources, such as heritage and museums, more effectively to develop skills on top of their existing skills, disadvantaged groups become more disadvantaged as they don't have the skills or educational background to use these resources (see Dawson 2019). Throughout this Element, I argue that museums and heritage sites should prioritise these disadvantaged groups and offer skills development to close this gap. Skills development is also strongly linked to the redistribution and recognition dimensions of social justice because redistribution is about getting an equal share of the knowledge and cultural resources and where one's exist-ence is also recognised so that they can have a voice and take part in controlling these resources. A few museums' skills development programmes are very useful and could be expanded through strong community partnerships, with more diverse people taking part in these programmes. The British Museum's training programme, 'The Trainee Experience', funded by the National Lottery Heritage Fund, is a good example to demonstrate how offering a skills devel-opment programme can also contribute to the parity of participation. The British Museum training programme[37] aimed to improve the skills of people from diverse backgrounds so that they could join the museum sector and be a part of the decision-making process.

Here, I would like to demonstrate the importance of skills development from heritage site research by discussing the case study of the European Commission–funded Emotive storytelling for cultural heritage project that conducted research in Turkey, the United Kingdom and Greece to develop effective digital tools for heritage and museum professionals and to engage with the public more effectively. In the research conducted in Turkey, with team members from University of York, we worked at the archaeological site, Çatalhöyük, which is UNESCO World Heritage Site and mostly known because of its early Neolithic settlement and egalitarian lifestyle (see Hodder and Marciniak 2015). In 2019, we went to Çatalhöyük to test and evaluate on- and offsite digital educational kits and 3D critical dialogue facilitation programmes. These tests and evaluations involved recruiting participants from nearby vil-lages to test and evaluate our programme, which also involved initial tests,

---

[37] See www.britishmuseum.org/our-work/national/skills-sharing-and-expertise/museum-futures.

evaluation/impact questionnaires following experiencing the programmes and follow-ups.

However, we didn't conduct the research with just our team members; we also recruited people from the nearby villages to work as researchers in our fieldwork (Figures 16 and 17). The young local researchers were given training about the research and how to use digital tools and conduct research, and they took part in every stage of research. They were also empowered to conduct the research on their own and interpret the results of data collection. While these local researchers learned how to use, for example, digital and research tools, they also became part of an international research team that recognised their contribution to the research. The training and skills development and taking part in an international research not only made them empowered but they also learned how to use heritage and museum spaces as a resource and take an equal share from these cultural resources. Although this is a very small-scale example, given that the research was conducted in south central Turkey, which

Figure 16 Emotive project at Çatalhöyük. Local researchers are testing digital tools

Figure 17 Local researchers running critical dialogue sessions with participants at the museum centre

is economically and educationally deprived (Apaydin 2016b), this demonstrates that a research project can still contribute to the skills development of local people, whatever their circumstances.

In addition, the perspectives and contributions of the local researchers not only decolonised the heritage research but it also boosted the data and, most importantly, enabled us as researchers to recognise different voices, give access to data to local people and to redistribute the knowledge to communities, first hand via the local researchers. As such, the focus of museum and heritage site work, projects and research should focus on how inequalities can be decreased through offering communities a range of platforms and opportunities to be able to participate equally in social, economic, cultural and political life. This is one of the main reasons that Arnstein's (1969) participation ladder, which I will discuss in Section 4.4.3 especially with regards to 'citizen power' that includes citizen control, delegated power and partnership model, becomes more important when redistributing knowledge and skills equally, recognising and acknowledging individuals and groups needs as well as for parity of participation, managing and decision-making processes of museums and heritage sites.

4.4.3 Community Partnership and Power Sharing

In the last two decades, community engagement through museums or heritage sites has become quite common; however, most of the engagement strategies are lacking in terms of exposing the dynamics, priorities and needs of those communities who have been engaged. One of the main reasons for that, I argue, is that the concept of community has not yet been fully explored and responded by researchers and professionals. Although communities play, or should play, a central role in any museum, especially from the perspective of developing strategies for planning and policies, the concept of the community has not been fully delved into (see Crooke 2007). Although the concept of community is perhaps difficult to define because it is an abstract concept and it has a variety of meanings, values and interpretations that differ in every part of the world, it can be defined as a group of people who shares and develops values and tries to preserve them to survive. However, these values distinguish communities from others and create boundaries between them. The concept of community is particularly significant for community museums and becomes more important for sustainability and the development of local communities. Developing sustainable community partnerships through museums and heritage sites is not only important for community development but it also is one of the main principles of social justice, which seeks equal redistribution of knowledge, recognition of diversities and representation in decision-making, as discussed at the beginning of this section. However, the type of community partnership I am advocating for is not simply consulting or getting the views of communities on projects, works and exhibitions. Rather, it involves critically and collaboratively designing and developing projects together, from the beginning of the museum or heritage project. This way, community members have a place in the decision-making process, develop skills and actively contribute to the community development and sustainability.

Hackney Museum's projects[38] that focus on reflecting the diverse histories and communities of the district are good examples demonstrating community-centred projects that have diverse and disadvantaged communities in developing projects collaboratively. For instance, the London Museums Hub refugee heritage projects (2004–2007) where refugee and migrant stories were collected through objects and used as educational resources; the 'Abolition of the trans-atlantic slave trade' (2007) project that collaborated with the African-Caribbean community in Hackney, leading to an exhibition, documentary and a theatre performance; 'Mapping the change 2010-2012' that recorded the impact of the London Olympics on local people's lives. The project took four years and brought together the diverse voices of Hackney's communities. It worked with more than 5,000 people across Hackney, including local community groups, individuals and artists who collaboratively produced the exhibition, film, audio records and photographic collection. A similar project: 'Sharing our

[38] See https://hackney-museum.hackney.gov.uk/projects/.

Stories – Exploring Jewish Stamford Hill 1930-1960' (2016) that collaborated with the Jewish community in Stamford Hill to explore long history of migration of Hackney and the Jewish experience within this process. These case studies and many more demonstrate not only how museums can work with diverse community groups and members but also, as part of a critical collaboration, it brings the dynamics of communities, authentic knowledge and interpretation into museum projects as community members are able to contribute to these projects.

Although Hackney Museum is very people centred, the questions about the long-term viability of partnerships between community groups and museums and how extensive and sustainable community partnership can shift power to people from institutions and organisations still remain unanswered in the heritage and museum context in many regions (see also Lynch 2016), or there are difficulties because of organisational structure (Simon 2010). The partnership should be sustainable and empower community members, who can then take roles in social and cultural life.

Sherry Arnstein (1969, 126), who developed a citizen participation ladder (Figure 18) that is often used in city planning and architectural studies, points out that "participation without redistribution of power is an empty and frustrating process for the powerless". This is similar to Nancy Fraser's argument on representation and parity of participation as part of the social justice framework. Collaboration with community groups at museums and heritage sites is quite common as discussed previously, however, the Arnstein's ladder has a great potential to make museum and heritage site partnerships more effective as well as ethical, more bottom-up and people centred in order to maintain sustainable partnerships and critical collaboration.

Although 'citizen power', which includes citizen control, delegated power and partnership, is an emerging practice in heritage sites and museums, giving power to community members to shape and direct museums and heritage work is one of the entanglements in heritage and museums. The last two, 'tokenism' and 'nonparticipation', are approaches that are quite common in the heritage and museum settings. For instance, in the heritage and museum context, the tokenistic approach has been used for a long time. Here placation means that although stakeholders or community members have a place to express their opinions, for example, about displays, the final decisions are taken by museum staff. Similarly, in the informing aspect, community members are informed about the projects but are not allowed to contribute to the decision-making process. This is similar to the consultation process where opinions are taken but not considered in the decision-making process. This can often be seen in the process of selecting World Heritage Sites by UNESCO where community

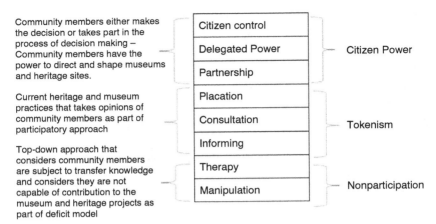

Figure 18 Sherry Arnstein's citizen participation ladder in relation to heritage and museums

members are informed, allowed to express their opinions and consulted on certain aspects, but they are considered as passive agents in the decision-making processes. This is similar to the top-down approaches that are still implemented in many parts of the world in the heritage and museum context; this approach doesn't explore community needs, dynamics and priorities.

What is important in Arnstein's ladder of participation is that, similar to Fraser's representation dimension of social justice, 'citizen power' includes dimensions of citizen control, delegated power and partnership. These three dimensions are also important when using museums and heritage sites as 'spaces' where inequalities and injustices can be overcome. In the heritage and museum context, 'citizen control' would be represented by community members developing ideas, for example, in exhibitions and educational and learning resources, where content is also developed by community members. The role of museum staff here is to not intervene with the project ideas but to support and give professional advice. 'Delegated power' is the sharing of the power between community groups and museums, where decisions are taken equally. 'Partnership' also represents power sharing between the museum and community members who are actively involved in the decision-making processes.

In other words, the type of community partnership that I've been advocating is based on power sharing with community members, who are then able to use museums and heritage sites as spaces where they actively shape, reshape and transform, reflecting their needs and priorities, as well as transforming for future directions. This, without doubt, would reduce inequalities and injustices because strong community partnerships would be based on the 'parity of participation' between community groups (see Fraser 2013). Finally, museums and heritage sites could serve as spaces where disadvantaged community groups can also use this space for developing skills and be a part of social, political and economic life.

5 Conclusion

In this research, I have explored and analysed the potential of heritage sites and museums to tackle inequalities and injustices using a social justice heritage and museum practice by taking an interdisciplinary approach, analysing and presenting discourses of inequalities and injustices and theoretical foundations of social justice and case studies. In most cases, museum and heritage practices and education programmes focus on preserving the material culture and heritage of the past and on using heritage sites and museums as spaces to transfer knowledge and implementing the agendas of curators and educators.

Heritage and museum researchers and practitioners need to think about social justice as a 'goal and process' (Bell 2016, 1), which requires critical people-centred approaches and methods to make social change by engaging in social, political and economic issues, as well as the needs and priorities of people (see also Chynoweth et al. 2020). This process involves equal participation in power sharing, not excluding any identity or economic groups, and engaging them mutually and equally to meet their needs, considering their diversities, differences and agencies (Bell 2016, 1). It also involves identifying and engaging with those who need support to develop themselves to participate equally, from the distribution of social, economic and cultural life related to the 'redistribution', 'recognition' and 'representation' dimensions of social justice. Tackling inequalities and injustices and decreasing oppressive forces for especially disadvantaged groups requires a strong and effective social justice approach. Critical consciousness needs to be developed – engaging with legitimate narratives and power in organisations and developing counter contemporary narratives to challenge this power, engaging with disadvantaged communities through building strong and sustainable partnerships to enable them to develop skills and empower them to use these cultural settings so that they can develop cultural, social and economic capital.

Lee Anne Bell (2016), a critical education theorist, develops social justice principles for educational settings by focusing on 'developing critical consciousness, deconstructing the binaries, developing counter narratives, analysing power, following oppressed people' (and more, see Bell 2016). I argue that these are strongly linked in the heritage and museum context and offer a way to develop critical and social justice heritage and museum practices, from designing and developing curatorial works and education programmes to participatory decision-making processes. The concept of 'critical consciousness' was developed by Paulo Freire (1970) in the context of helping Brazilian working classes be aware of social and political inequalities and injustices, and taking actions themselves to change their own situation. Critical consciousness aims to help individuals understand the discourses of inequalities and injustices (see also Bell 2016). In the heritage and museum context, the critical consciousness process can be applied well in all curatorial and education programmes, especially through storytelling (see Bell 2010), using material culture to understand historical and contemporary issues that created or helped to create inequalities and injustices. Developing critical consciousness, in displays and the content of education programmes and learning resources, rather than transferring knowledge, has the potential to negotiate and raise empathy for difficult histories that groups and communities have had or to present the histories of alternative societies, as in the case of the curatorial and educational works of Hackney Museum and Emotive project discussed in previous sections.

Critical consciousness is also strongly linked to developing counter-narratives against the official and 'legitimate' knowledge that is often seen in undemocratic, authoritarian and oppressive regimes and countries. Discrimination, exclusion, categorising and privilege are some ways that some groups exclude others and are perhaps the most common tools of oppression. This can be seen in the binaries of "black/white, straight/gay, male/female, young/old, disabled/non-disabled" (Bell 2016, 19), and wealthy/poor, educated/non-educated that we all come cross in everyday life. This issue has been well researched and analysed in social sciences and artists and activists reflected for a long time on this (see Bell 2016). The positive impact of counter-narratives, for example, can be seen in recent history, such as with the abolition slavery, extending voting rights to women and rights for different identity groups, such as LGBTQ+ (Bell 2016, 19).

Heritage sites and museums are especially significant places where these binaries can be deconstructed and to create a more inclusive approach by using their collections, displays and in the content of educational and learning resources. Many museums in Europe have archaeological and contemporary collections from all over the world, so they have the material and resources to demonstrate alternative pasts and social lives where categorisation and exclusion did not exist (or, at least, in radically different ways from today), where different colours and sexual orientation did not matter, where there were no wealthy and poor people and where everyone was treated equally, which is also strongly linked to developing and applying counter-narratives in heritage and museum practices. Throughout this research, I have emphasised and considered heritage and museums as spaces where different identity groups can get into contact and learn about differences and diversities to prevent prejudices and to develop empathy. Heritage sites and museums perhaps are the most capable institutions and organisations to develop counter-narratives because they hold the material culture of the past and present needed to develop counter stories. This is strongly linked to, of course, the interpretation stages of material culture and heritage at the sites and museums and requires a strong people-centred approach rather than expert knowledge. It needs to consider individual and collective stories that relate to the material culture where meanings are ascribed, values and memories are developed.

In Section 4, I discussed community partnerships and power sharing and its dynamics. However, *analysing power* in terms of using heritage and museum spaces in conjunction with community needs and priorities is crucial when working towards people-centred social justice heritage practice. Bell (2016, 20) emphasises that it is important to analyse power to find out

> ... in whose interest do systems operate? Who benefits and who pays? ... to reveal how power operates through normalizing relations of domination by presenting certain ideas and practices as rational and self-evident, as part of the natural order. Once people begin to question what has previously been taken for granted, the way is open to imagine new possibilities and practices.

Considering that in heritage and museum institutions, power operates through a top-down approach where ideas and interests are developed in conjunction with expert agendas and then implemented to communities, the ethical question arises as to how this structure can be overturned and shifted towards the community interest and ideas? The research of Paulo Freire (1970), based on 'participatory action research' or a strong ethnographic approach and methodologies, worked towards developing a heritage practice that has the potential to deconstruct organisational power, as I discussed in Section 3. In this way, heritage and museum experts can avoid imposing their own agendas during the decision-making process.

For museums and heritage sites, working with diverse groups is another critical and crucial aspect towards developing social justice approaches to overcome inequalities and injustices as well as to prevent biases, prejudice and all forms of racism. This aspect is also linked to Allport's contact theory. Working with different and diverse groups not only would make heritage and museums more people centred, but would also bring groups and communities together so that they get to know each other. It would raise empathy and sympathy and they would work together towards social justice by deconstructing power relations and overcoming oppressive forces. Bell (2016) uses the BLM movement, which illustrates how diverse groups can work together against injustices and inequalities. Hackney Museum's project, 'Hello Cazenova', is another example of working with diverse groups and building solidarity between communities.

Heritage and museums are certainly progressing and taking more responsibility in terms of social issues through developing new approaches and methods. This can be seen in many museums and heritage practices, as discussed throughout this Element. However, inequalities and injustices are also increasing and in many parts of the world, disadvantaged groups are becoming more deprived, unequal access to resources is rising, discrimination against many different identity and diverse groups is increasing and the social and economic environment is changing. Therefore, heritage sites and museums should focus on what approaches and methodologies can be developed to engage with the changing the world and the issues of increasing inequalities in order to make positive change. This is, of course, very challenging and requires heritage and museum researchers and practitioners to think in more innovative ways. However, as I attempted to demonstrate in this research, heritage and museums are powerful spaces, 'micro-organisations', with the ability to make change because they have a direct link to communities and people.

References

Adichie, C. N. (2009). The Danger of a Single Story. TED Talks. TEDGlobal2009. https://www.ted.com/talks/chimamanda_ngozi_adichie_the_danger_of_a_single_story?language=en.

Ahmed, S. (2012). *On Being Included: Racism and Diversity in Institutional Life*. Durham: Duke University Press.

Akçam, T. (2004). *From Empire to Republic: Turkish Nationalism and the Armenian Genocide*. London: Zed Books.

Akdar, A. (2000). *Varlık Vergisi Ve Türkleştirme Politikaları*. Istanbul: Iletişim Yayınları.

Allport, W. G. (1954). *The Nature of Prejudice*. Reading: Addison-Wesley.

Anderson, B. (2006). *Imagined Communities: Reflections on the Origin and Spread of Nationalism*. London: Verso.

Apaydin, V. (2016a). 'The Challenge of Neoliberalism and Archaeological Heritage in Turkey: Protection or Destruction?' In P. Aparicio-Resco (ed.), *Archaeology and Neoliberalism*. Madrid: JAS Arqueologia. 341–52.

Apaydin, V. (2016b). 'Economic Rights, Heritage Sites and Communities: Sustainability and Protection'. *Complutum*, 27(2), 369–84.

Apaydin, V. (2016c). 'Effective or Not? Success or Failure? Assessing Heritage and Archaeological Education Programmes – The Case of Çatalhöyük'. *International Journal of Heritage Studies*, 22(10), 828–43.

Apaydin, V. (2018). 'The Entanglement of the Heritage Paradigm: Values, Meanings and Uses'. *International Journal of Heritage Studies*, 24(5), 491–507.

Apaydin, V. (2020a). *Critical Perspectives on Cultural Memory and Heritage: Construction, Transformation and Destruction*. London: UCL Press.

Apaydin, V. (2020b). 'Heritage, Memory and Social Justice: Reclaiming Space and Identity'. In V. Apaydin (ed.), *Critical Perspectives on Cultural Memory and Heritage: Construction, Transformation and Destruction*. London: UCL Press. 84–97.

Appadurai, A. (1995). 'The Production of Locality'. In R. Fardon (ed.), *Counterworks: Managing the Diversity of Knowledge*. London: Routledge. 204–25.

Apple, M. W. (2004). *Ideology and Curriculum*. New York: Routledge.

Apple, M. W., Au, W. and Gandin, L. A. (eds.). (2009). *The Routledge International Handbook of Critical Education*. New York: Routledge.

Arnstein, S. (1969). 'A Ladder of Citizen Participation'. *Journal of the American Institute of Planners*, 35(4), 216–24.

Ashworth, G. J., Graham, B. and Tunbridge, J. E. (2007). *Pluralising Pasts: Heritage, Identity and Place in Multicultural Societies*. London: Pluto Press.

Atakuman, C. (2008). 'Cradle or Crucible: Anatolia and Archaeology in the Early Years of the Turkish Republic (1923–1938)'. *Journal of Social Archaeology*, 8, 214–35.

Bakhtin, M. M. (1981). *The Dialogic Imagination Four Essays*. Austin: University of Texas Press.

Baraldi, B. S., Shoup, D. and Zan,L. (2013). 'Understanding Cultural Heritage in Turkey: Institutional Context and Organizational Issues'. *International Journal of Heritage Studies*, 19(7), 728–48.

Basu, P. (2021). 'Re-mobilising Colonial Collections in Decolonial Times: Exploring the Latent Possibilities of N. W. Thomas's West African Collections'. In F. Driver, M. Nesbitt and C. Cornish (eds.), *Mobile Museums: Collections in Circulation*. London: UCL Press. 44–70.

Baum, F., Newman, L. and Biedrzycki, K. (2014). 'Vicious Cycles: Digital Technologies and Determinants of Health in Australia'. *Health Promotion International*, 29(2), 349–60.

Beaunoyer, E., Dupéré, S. and Guitton, J. M. (2020). 'COVID-19 and Digital Inequalities: Reciprocal Impacts and Mitigation Strategies'. *Computer in Human Behavior*, 111. https://doi.org/10.1016/j.chb.2020.106424.

Bell, L. A. (2010). *Storytelling for Social Justice: Connecting Narrative and the Arts in Antiracist Teaching*. New York : Routledge.

Bell, L. A. (2016). 'Theoretical Foundations for Social Justice Education'. In M. Adams and L. A. Bell with D. J. Goodman and K. Y. Joshi (eds.), *Teaching for Diversity and Social Justice*, 3rd ed. New York: Routledge. 3–26.

Bennett, T. (1995). *The Birth of the Museum: History, Theory, Politics*. London: Routledge.

Bennett, T. (2004). *Pasts Beyond Memory: Evolution, Museums, Colonialism*. London: Routledge.

Bennett, T. (2017). *Museum, Power, Knowledge: Selected Essays*. London: Routledge.

Bennett, T., Cameron, F., Dias, N. et al. (2017). *Collecting, Ordering, Governing: Anthropology, Museums, and Liberal Government*. Durham: Duke University Press.

Bennett, T., Savage, M. and Silva, E. (2009). *Culture, Class, Distinction*. London: Routledge.

Boast, R. (2011). 'Neocolonial Collaboration: Museum as Contact Zone Revisited'. *Museum Anthropology*, 34(1), 56–70.

Borck, L. (2019). 'Constructing the Future History: Prefiguration as Historical Epistemology and the Chronopolitics of Archaeology'. *Journal of Contemporary Archaeology*, 5(2), 229–38.

Borg, C. and Mayo, P. (2010). 'Museums: Adult Education as Cultural Politics'. *New Directions for Adult and Continuing Education*, 2010(127), 35–44.

Bourdieu, P. (1984). *Distinction: A Social Critique of the Judgement of Taste*. London: Routledge.

Bourdieu, P. (1986). 'The Forms of Capital'. In J. Richardson (ed.), *Handbook of Theory and Research for the Sociology of Education*. New York: Greenwood. 241–58.

Bourdieu, P. (2005). 'Habitus'. In J. Hillier and E. Rooksby (eds.), *Habitus: A Sense of Place*. Aldershot: Ashgate. 43–52.

Brown, W. (2019). *In the Ruins of Neoliberalism: The Rise of Antidemocratic Politics in the West*. New York: Columbia University Press.

Brusius, M. (2020). '100 Histories of 100 Worlds in One Object'. *German Historical Institute London Bulletin*, 42(1), 103–11.

Butler, B. (2006). 'Heritage and the Present Past'. In C. Tilley, W. Keane, S. Küchler, M. Rowlands and P. Spyer (eds.), *Handbook of Material Culture*. London: Sage. 463–79.

Çakir Ilhan, A. (2009). 'Educational Studies in Turkish Museum'. *Procedia – Social and Behavioural Sciences*, 1(1), 342–6.

Calvert, A. and Warren, M. E. (2014). 'Deliberative Democracy and Framing Effects: Why Frames are a Problem and How Deliberative Minipublics Might Overcome Them'. In K. Grönlund, A. Bächtinger and M. Setälä (eds.), *Deliberative Mini-Publics: Involving Citizens in the Democratic Process*. Colchester: ECPR Press. 203–24.

Christen, K. (2006). 'Ara Irititja: Protecting the Past, Accessing the Future – Indigenous Memories in a Digital Age'. *Museum Anthropology*, 29(1), 56–60.

Chynoweth, A., Lynch, B., Petersen, K. and Smed, S. (eds.). (2020). *Museums and Social Change: Challenging the Unhelpful Museum*. London: Routledge.

Clifford, J. (1997). 'Museums as Contact Zones'. In J. Clifford (ed.), *Routes: Travel and Translation in the Late Twentieth Century*. Cambridge, MA: Harvard University Press. 188–219.

Coffee, K. (2008). 'Cultural Inclusion, Exclusion and the Formative Roles of Museums'. *Museum Management and Curatorship*, 23(3), 261–79.

Cohen, A. (1985). *The Symbolic Construction of Community*. London: Routledge.

Crooke, E. (2007). *Museums and Community: Ideas, Issues and Challenges*. New York: Routledge.

Dawson, E. (2014). '"Not Designed for Us": How Science Museums and Science Centers Socially Exclude Low-Income, Minority Ethnic Groups'. *Science Education*, 98(6), 981–1008. https://doi.org/10.1002/sce.21133.

Dawson, E. (2019). *Equity, Exclusion and Everyday Science Learning: The Experiences of Minoritised Groups*. London: Routledge.

Denton, K. A. (2014). *Exhibiting the Past: Historical Memory and the Politics of Museums in Postsocialist China*. Honolulu: University of Hawaii Press.

Deuze, D. (2006). 'Participation, Remediation, Bricolage: Considering Principal Components of a Digital Culture'. *The Information Society*, 22(2), 63–75.

Dewey, J. (1954). *Democracy and Education*. New York : Macmillan Company.

Dibley, B. (2005). 'The Museum's Redemption: Contact Zones, Government and the Limits of Reform'. *International Journal of Cultural Studies*, 8(1), 5–27.

Drotner, K., Dziekan, V., Parry, R. and Schrøder, K. (2018). *The Routledge Handbook of Museums, Media and Communication*. London: Routledge.

Endacott, J. L. and Brooks, S. (2013). 'An Updated Theoretical and Practical Model for Promoting Historical Empathy'. *Social Studies Research and Practice*, 8(1), 41–58.

Estes, N. (2019). *Our History is the Future: Standing Rock versus the Dakota Access Pipeline, and the Long Tradition of Indigenous Resistance*. London: Verso.

Evans, H. and Rowlands, M. J. (eds.). (2021). *Grassroots Values and Local Cultural Heritage in China*. Lanham: Lexington Books.

Falk, H. J. and Dierking, D. L. (2018). *Learning from Museums*. Lanham: Rowman & Littlefield.

Fraser, N. (1987). 'Women, Welfare and the Politics of Need Interpretation'. *Thesis Eleven*, 17(1): 88–106.

Fraser, N. (1997). *Justice Interruptus: Critical Reflections on the Post-Socialist Condition*. New York: Routledge.

Fraser, N. (1998). 'Social Justice in the Age of Identity Politics: Redistribution, Recognition, Participation'. Pdf https://www.ssoar.info/ssoar/bitstream/handle/document/12624/ssoar-1998-fraser-social_justice_in_the_age.pdf?sequence=1.

Fraser, N. (2000). 'Rethinking Recognition'. *New Left Review*, 3, 107–20.

Fraser, N. (2003). 'Social Justice in the Age of Identity Politics: Redistribution, Recognition and Participation'. In N. Fraser and A. Honneth (eds.), *Redistribution or Recognition? A Political-Philosophical Exchange*. London: Verso. 7–88.

Fraser, N. (2009). *Scales of Justice: Reimagining Political Space in a Globalizing World*. New York: Columbia University Press.

Fraser, N. (2013). *Fortunes of Feminism: From State-Managed Capitalism to Neoliberal Crisis*. London: Verso.

Freire, P. (1970). *Pedagogy of the Oppressed*. New York: Continuum.

Freire, P. and Macedo, P. D. (1995). 'A Dialogue: Culture, Language, and Race'. *Harvard Educational Review*, 65(3), 377–402.

Girard, M. (2015). 'What Heritage Tells Us About the Turkish State and Turkish Society'. *European Journal of Turkish Studies* [Online]. http://journals.openedition.org/ejts/5227.

Gouriévidis, L. (ed.). (2014). *Museums and Migration: History, Memory and Politics*. London: Routledge.

Graeber, D. and Wengrow, D. (2021). *The Dawn of Everything: A New History of Humanity*. London: Allen Lane.

Gramsci, A. (1971). *Selections from the Prison Notebooks* (Q. Hoare and G. N. Smith, trans.). New York: International.

Hackney Museum (2017). Disability and access projects. Recent project case studies (Written by Emma Wick) https://hackney-museum.hackney.gov.uk/projects/ https://drive.google.com/file/d/1xyHEqz2QCjhWtB-F6DunCsgyySvweFFy/view.

Harrison, R. (2013). *Heritage: Critical Approaches*. London: Routledge.

Harvey, D. (2005). *A Brief History of Neoliberalism*. Oxford: Oxford University Press.

Harvey, D. (2007). 'Neoliberalism as Creative Destruction'. *The Annals of the American Academy of Political and Social Science*, 610, 22–44.

Harvey, D. (2009). *Social Justice and the City*. Athens: University of Georgia Press.

Hein, G. E. (2005). 'The Role of Museums in Society: Education and Social Action'. *Curator*, 48(4), 357–63.

Hein, G. E. (2012). *Progressive Museum Practice: John Dewey and Democracy*. London: Routledge.

Hewison, R. (1987). *The Heritage Industry: Britain in a Climate of Decline*. London: Methuen.

Hodder, I. and Marciniak, A. (eds.). (2015). *Assembling Çatalhöyük*. Leeds: Maney.

Hollowell, J. and Nicholas, G. (2009). 'Using Ethnographic Methods to Articulate Community-Based Conceptions of Cultural Heritage Management'. *Public Archaeology*, 8(2–3), 141–60.

Hood, M. (2004). 'Staying Away: Why People Choose to Not Visit Museums'. In G. Anderson (ed.), *Reinventing the Museum: Historical and Contemporary Perspectives on the Paradigm Shift*. Walnut Creek: AltaMira Press. 150–7.

Hooper-Greenhill, E. (2007). *Museums and Education: Purpose, Pedagogy, Performance*. London: Routledge.

Horniman Museums and Gardens (2020). 'Climate and Ecology Manifesto January 2020'. https://www.horniman.ac.uk/wp-content/uploads/2020/02/horniman-climate-manifesto-final-29-jan-2020.pdf.

Ipsos MORI. (2011). *Glasgow Household Survey*. Scotland: Glasgow City Council.

Janes, R. R. and Sandell, R. (eds.). (2019). *Museum Activism*. Abingdon: Routledge.

Joy, C. (2020). *Heritage Justice*. Cambridge: Cambridge University Press.

Kidd, J. (2014). *Museums in the New Mediascape: Transmedia, Participation, Ethics*. Surrey: Ashgate.

Kidd, J., Cairns, S., Drago, S., Ryall, A. and Stearn, M. (eds.). (2017). *Challenging History in the Museum: International Perspectives*. London: Routledge.

Kınıkoğlu, N. C. (2021). 'Displaying the Ottoman Past in an "Old" Museum of a "New" Turkey: The Topkapi Palace Museum'. *Southeast European and Black Sea Studies*, 21(4), 549–69.

Kinsley, P. R. (2016). 'Inclusion in Museums: A Matter of Social Justice'. *Museum Management and Curatorship*, 31(5), 474–90.

Kolb, D. (1984). *Experiential Learning: Experience as the Source of Learning and Development*. London: Prentice-Hall.

Lang, C. and Reeve, J. (eds.). (2018). *New Museum Practice in Asia*. London: Lund Humphries.

Lefebvre, H. (1991). *The Production of Space*. Oxford: Blackwell.

Lynch, B. (2011). *Whose Cake is it Anyway? A Collaborative Investigation into Engagement and Participation in 12 Museums and Galleries in the UK*. Summary Report. London: Paul Hamlyn Foundation.

Lynch, B. (2014). 'Whose Cake is it Anyway? Museums, Civil Society and the Changing Reality of Public Engagement'. In L. Gourievidis (ed.), *Museums and Migration: History, Memory and Politics*. London: Routledge. 67–80.

Lynch, B. (2016). 'Good for You, But I Don't Care!'. In C. Mörsch, A. Sachs and T. Sieber (eds.), *Contemporary Curating and Museum Education*. Bielefeld: transcript Verlag. 255–68.

Lynch, B. (2021). 'Introduction: Neither Helpful nor Unhelpful – A Clear Way Forward for the Useful Museum'. In A. Chynoweth, B. Lynch, K. Petersen and S. Smed (eds.), *Museums and Social Change: Challenging the Unhelpful Museum*. London: Routledge. 1–32.

Lynch, T. and Alberti, J. M. M. S. (2010). 'Legacies of Prejudice: Racism, Co-production and Radical Trust in the Museum'. *Museum Management and Curatorship*, 25(1), 13–35.

Macdonald, S. (ed.). (2006). *Companion to Museum Studies*. New York: Wiley-Blackwell.

Mason, R. (2008). 'Be Interested and Beware: Joining Economic Valuation and Heritage Conservation'. *International Journal of Heritage Studies*, 14(4), 303–18.

Mazzanti, M. (2003). 'Valuing Cultural Heritage in a Multi-Attribute Framework Microeconomic Perspectives and Policy Implications'. *Journal of Socio-Economics*, 32, 549–69.

McKinney, S. (2018). Generating Pre-Historical Empathy: An Examination of a Digital Classroom Kit. Unpublished MSc Thesis, University of York.

McLaren, P. (1997). *Revolutionary Multiculturalism: Pedagogies of Dissent for the New Millennium*. Boulder: Westview Press.

Merriman, N. (1991). *Beyond the Glass Case: The Past, the Heritage and the Public in Britain*. Leicester: Leicester University Press.

Meskell, L. (2018). *A Future in Ruins: UNESCO, World Heritage, and the Dream of Peace*. New York: Oxford University Press.

Mihelj, S., Leguina, A. and Downey, J. (2019). 'Culture is Digital: Cultural Participation, Diversity and the Digital Divide'. *New Media & Society*, 21(7), 1465–85.

Miller, D. (ed.). (2005). *Materiality*. Durham: Duke University Press.

Miller, D. (2009). *The Comfort of Things*. Cambridge: Polity.

Nicholas, G. and Smith, C. (2020). 'Considering the Denigration and Destruction of Indigenous Heritage as Violence'. In V. Apaydin (ed.), *Critical Perspectives on Cultural Memory and Heritage*. London: UCL Press. 131–54.

O'Neill, M. (2021). *Are Museums Failing Those Who Need Support Most?* Learning and Engagement. Museum Associations. www.museumsassociation.org/category/learning-and-engagement/.

Posocco, L. (2018). 'Nationalism, Politics, and Museums in Turkey under the Justice and Development Party (AKP): The Case of the Panorama Museum 1453'. *Contemporary Southeastern Europe*, 5(1), 35–55.

Robinson, L., Cotten, R. S., Ono, H. et al. (2015). 'Digital Inequalities and Why They Matter'. *Information, Communication & Society*, 18(5), 569–82.

Ronayne, M. (2005). *The Cultural and Environmental Impact of Large Dams in Southeast Turkey*. London: Kurdish Human Rights Project and National University of Ireland.

Rossman, G. and Peterson, R. (2015). 'The Instability of Omnivorous Cultural Taste Over Time'. *Poetics*, 52, 139–53.

Rowley, S., Schaepe, D., Sparrow, L. et al. (2010). 'Building an On-Line Research Community: The Reciprocal Research Network'. www.archimuse.com/mw2010/papers/rowley/rowley.html.

Said, E. W. (1994).*Culture & Imperialism*. London: Vintage.

Sandell, R. (2003). 'Social Inclusion, the Museum and the Dynamics of Sectoral Change'. *Museum & Society*, 191, 45–62.

Sandell, R. and Nightingale, E. (eds.). (2012). *Museums, Equality and Social Justice*. London: Routledge.

Schofield, J. (ed.). (2016). *Who Needs Experts? Counter-mapping Cultural Heritage*. London: Routledge.

Silberman, N. (2007). '"Sustainable" Heritage? Public Archaeological Interpretation and Marketed Past'. In Y. Hamilakis and P. Duke (eds.), *Archaeology and Capitalism: From Ethics to Politics*. Walnut Creek: Left Coast Press. 179–94.

Simon, N. (2010). *The Participatory Museum*. Santa Cruz: Museum 2.0.

Smith, C., Burke, H., Ralph, J. et al. (2019). 'Pursuing Social Justice through Collaborative Archaeologies in Aboriginal Australia'. *Archaeologies*, 15, 536–69.

Smith, L. (2006). *Uses of Heritage*. London: Routledge.

Smith, L. (2021). *Emotional Heritage: Visitor Engagement at Museums and Heritage Sites*. New York: Routledge.

Tallon, L. and Walker, K. (eds.). (2008). *Digital Technologies and the Museum Experience*. Plymouth: AltaMira Press.

Tuik (Turkiye Istatistik Kurumu) (2020). Kütürel Miras 2019. https://data .tuik.gov.tr/Bulten/Index?p=Kulturel-Miras-2019-33633.

Tureli, I. (2014). 'Heritagisation of the "Ottoman/Turkish House" in the 1970s: Istanbul-Based Actors, Associations and Their Networks'. *European Journal of Turkish Studies*, 19, 1–32.

Turtle, J. and Turtle, M. (2020). 'Rewriting the Script: Power and Change through a Museum of Homelessness'. In A. Chynoweth, B. Lynch, K. Petersen and S. Smed (eds.), *Museums and Social Change: Challenging the Unhelpful Museum*. New York: Routledge. 48–59.

Watts, N. F. (2010). *Activists in Office: Kurdish Politics and Protest in Turkey*. Seattle: University of Washington Press.

Were, G. (2014). 'Digital Heritage, Knowledge Networks, and Source Communities: Understanding Digital Objects in a Melanesian Society'. *Museum Anthropology*, 37(2), 133–43.

Winter, T. (2013). 'Clarifying the Critical in Critical Heritage Studies'. *International Journal of Heritage Studies*, 19(6), 532–45. https://doi.org/10 .1080/13527258.2012.720997.

Witcomb, A. (2013). 'Understanding the Role of Affect in Producing a Critical Pedagogy for History Museums'. *Museum Management and Curatorship*, 28(3), 255–71.

Young, I. M. (1990). *Justice and the Politics of Difference*. Princeton: Princeton University Press.

Zencirci, G. (2014). 'Civil Society's History: New Constructions of Ottoman Heritage by the Justice and Development Party in Turkey'. *European Journal of Turkish Studies*, 19, 1–20.

Zhang, L. (2020). Jianchuan Museum Complex: Memory, Ethics and Power in Chinese Private Heritage Entrepreneurship. Unpublished Doctoral Thesis, UCL.

Zhu, Y. (2021). *Heritage Tourism: From Problems to Possibilities*. Cambridge: Cambridge University Press.

Acknowledgements

Throughout the years of research, I have benefited a lot from colleagues and friends all around the world. I owe a big thank you to Michael Rowlands, the series editor, for his guidance and help throughout all stages of this Element, without his support this Element wouldn't be possible. I owe a big thanks to Emma Wick, former heritage learning manager of Hackney Museum and Anna Newbury, current heritage learning manager of Hackney Museum for all their help and for providing resources at the Hackney Museum. I must also thank the peer reviewers who provided invaluable comments and suggestions. Thanks also to my colleagues at the Institute of Education, UCL, Art, Design & Museology: Claire Robins, Marquard Smith, Annie Davey, Andrew Ash, Caroline Marcus, Lesley Burgess, Thomas Jones, Pam Meecham, John Reeve, Josephine Borradaile, Sophie Huckfield and Ross Head. I would also like to thank the Art, Design and Museology students who helped me to more critically think about heritage over the years. Lastly, special thanks go to Jonathan Gardner, Sara Perry, Brenna Hassett, Beverley Butler, Louise Martin, Colin Sterling, Andrew Bevan, Beatrijs de Groot, Rachel King, Gabriel Moshenska, Ian Kirkpatrick, Paul Tourle, Jeff Marks, David Francis and Gwendoline Maurer, and of course my mum and dad.

Cambridge Elements ☰

Critical Heritage Studies

Kristian Kristiansen
University of Gothenburg

Michael Rowlands
UCL

Francis Nyamnjoh
University of Cape Town

Astrid Swenson
Bath University

Shu-Li Wang
Academia Sinica

Ola Wetterberg
University of Gothenburg

About the Series

This series focuses on the recently established field of Critical Heritage Studies. Interdisciplinary in character, it brings together contributions from experts working in a range of fields, including cultural management, anthropology, archaeology, politics, and law. The series will include volumes that demonstrate the impact of contemporary theoretical discourses on heritage found throughout the world, raising awareness of the acute relevance of critically analysing and understanding the way heritage is used today to form new futures.

Critical Heritage Studies

Printed in the USA
CPSIA information can be obtained
at www.ICGtesting.com
LVHW021240240823
756042LV00001B/79